PSYCHIC ADVENTURE

Psychic Adventure

MITCHELL BINGHAM

VANTAGE PRESS
New York Washington Atlanta Hollywood

FIRST EDITION

Published by Vantage Press, Inc.
516 West 34th Street, New York, New York 10001

Manufactured in the United States of America
Standard Book Number 533-03308-X

Dedicated to all those humans who have made an impact on me, both smooth and rough, and thus added to the adventure and experience of my life.

Contents

Introduction

I believe Eric Berne and Transactional Analysis have brought us into a new, exciting land whose extent we have hardly explored at all. In the same way that Freud and his followers opened up intoxicating new vistas with their discoveries of the realm of the unconscious, Transactional Analysis, or TA, goes some steps further.

This is based fundamentally on the postulate that we are not just one but many, that we have many so-called ego states, and that we switch from one to the other, often quite unexpectedly.

So that to talk about a person as "bad," as we so often do—You Are Not OK— is based on a false concept of the unity of the other. How much better to say: "I don't like what your Critical Parent is doing—I am frightened by your Vengeful Child!—Your Spunky Child is so bold, he sometimes makes me angry, as just now!"

Or calling her or him "good" while pleasant may not be as satisfactory as saying: "I love your Nurturing Parent; she makes me feel cared for!—When your Free Child laughs, I feel great!—The insights of your Little Professor inspire me, too!"

This book is not a scientific treatise. I'm not an expert. It's a personal account of my adventures in life, particularly what happened to my psyche or soul as I encountered various situations and stimuli. However, it's written from the TA standpoint which has given me enough perspective to overcome my quite considerable guilt or shame, and honesty to recount my experiences as I remember them.

You may get some insights into your own life—I hope so. They can come like flashes, one after another.

In order to elucidate some of the TA terms used in my story, there follow some introductory pages about Parent, Adult, Child, about the four basic life positions, about strokes, and so on. Of course, you may be one of the happy millions who have read "I'm OK—You're OK" or one of the other TA books, and then you may want to skip this introduction and get on with the tale itself.

The Ego States

Berne postulates that there are three basic ego states and that all the various states we get into are subdivisions of these main ones and not distinct.

They are, one: *Parent,* representing all the instructions, ideas and attitudes received from our parents and other figures to whom we've given authority during our childhood and as we grow throughout life. It represents the civilizing cement which in the past has helped to hold our society together. There are two main divisions of this ego state, viz.: the caring, nourishing part called *Nurturing Parent,* and the *Critical* or *Controlling Parent,* called also *Pig Parent.*

Two: *Adult.* Adult is the reasoning computer which takes in the input from the outside world and makes some kind of sense out of it. It doesn't feel or criticize, but advises and can lead if given the opportunity. It exists to serve the whole personality and not itself.

Three: *Child,* the seat of the emotions, passions and energy. What the young child starts with. It tends to reproduce and continue the reactions felt in childhood, hence the name. It has four main components which may have contradictory aims and solutions. As follows:

Adaptive Child is the element that feels fear and insecurity and hence for the sake of survival learns from parents and its surroundings and thus builds Parent and perhaps Adult also.

The *Little Professor* is the creative, bold, curious, intuitive part that comes close in my view to the supernatural, as does Nurturing Parent. It is well-named *Spunky* by Fanita English,

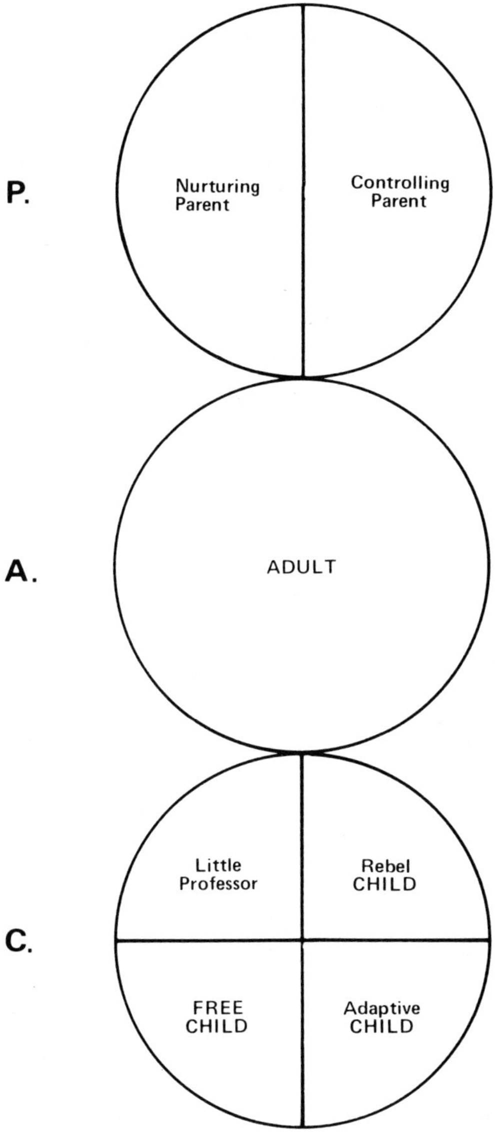

Figure 1—*The Ego States*

brilliant psychotherapist of Philadelphia.

Free Child is also called *Natural Child*, the *Princess* or *Prince*. This is the part that loves, needs care, and is close to what we commonly call "the heart." It laughs and experiences fun.

Rebellious or *Vengeful Child* arises as reaction to pain or deprivation—as we shall see in my own life. It seems to be the seat of anger.

Trying to diagram these ego states isn't easy as the diagrams are more like educated guesses than accurate maps. But they do help us to visualize what otherwise would become a burden on the mind.

This one (Figure 1) represents a fair summary of what the TA writers have used.

Strokes

In order to live, people need stimulation. The element of stimulation is called in TA a stroke, seemingly associated with feelings.

Strokes can go all the way from physical touching, a continuing pleasure which is essential for the survival of babies, to purely verbal, even written strokes. All the kinds of strokes give the message: You are a person whose existence I, the stroker, recognize and who is important enough to me that I give you this token of my recognition.

Strokes can be positive—involving good feelings, usually coming from the Nurturing or loving Parent, or from the Free, loving Child. Or they can be negative—involving bad feelings, which usually are given from Critical Parent or Vengeful, angry Child.

Children can't survive without any strokes. But all too many can and do survive on Negative ones.

I think it's fair to say that most people in our society suffer from not enough positive strokes. Claude Steiner, provocative pupil and follower of Eric Berne, calls this scarcity "The Stroke

Economy." He has an engaging way of expressing this truth in a story he calls "A Fuzzy Tale" contained in his book, *Scripts People Live*.

In this story a wicked witch persuades people that if they give away too many positive strokes called "Warm Fuzzies," these will run out and there won't be enough left for the strokers themselves. This fear spreads until a generous lady tells the children not to fear, the supply is unlimited.

The parallel between the situation of scarcity in this modern fairy tale and that in our society is strikingly apt.

I believe we live in a violent society, as many maintain, basically because in spite of our so-called comforts, our so-called civilization, it's a *form of violence* not to give all the good strokes each child and each person would like!

Humans are nurturing; mammals are nurturing. Half the human race have those lovely swelling breasts which haunt our dreams and typify the generous giving which is so natural and so right. Even if we men aren't so happily endowed, nurturing parenthood can come as naturally to us and be as rewarding.

I found this in the midst of hard work and a difficult marriage, as you will see.

On the other hand, in organizations, in therapy, in any relationships, the minute a person or a leader gets dominating or critical or loses his faith in the growth of the other person, he no longer can give positive strokes but reverts to the old authoritarian solutions and *violence* is being done. Alas, as we shall see in my own life, many people are addicted to negative strokes. They want and look for them, so Critical Parents flourish. Also many conditional strokes are given: you can be OK if . . . (you do it my way!).

Four Life Positions

A child soon begins to weigh herself or himself in relation to other people, the important source of the strokes he or she requires in order to live.

There are four fundamental life positions which express this relationship. These positions are taken in childhood in order to help us make a picture we can understand of the world, what's going on around us, and how we, with our burning desires, are treated.

We can move from one to another, sometimes we do quite often. But there's one in which we feel most at home, representing the basic decision we made early on and to which we usually return after a trip around the others.

These four are: I'm OK—You're OK; I'm OK—You're Not OK; I'm Not OK—You're OK; and I'm Not OK—You're Not OK. These four can be arranged in quadrants called "The OK Corral," as was worked out by Franklin Ernst, as in Fig. 2. This helps to visualize moving from one quadrant to another as you see I have done.

In whichever position most of us humans start—there is a question about this—it seems to me that most of us wind up in the *Vengeful* Quadrant: I'm OK—You/He/She/They Are Not OK, where Vengeful Child gives the motive power. Thomas Harris, author of *I'm OK—You're OK* assumes that a child takes this position to avoid the "awful void" of I'm Not OK into which he believes we come naturally as children because of our littleness and lack of power.

The favorite feelings and qualities associated with this position are anger, sarcasm, persecuted, judgmental, distrustful and hostile.

The obvious position we take when we're being punished, discounted or put down in one way or another *if* we go along with it is the Guilty one: I'm Not OK—You/She/He/They Are OK. This, encouraged by the obeying or compliant part of Adaptive Child is what makes conformists of millions of us and helps us to be good members of peer groups, organizations, armies or what have you.

The favorite feelings or qualities of this position are: worry, guilt, inadequacy, confusion, self-doubt.

The good and seemingly most healthy position is the *Equality* one: I'm OK—You're OK, into which according to Steiner we are naturally born. This is the Prince or Princess position in

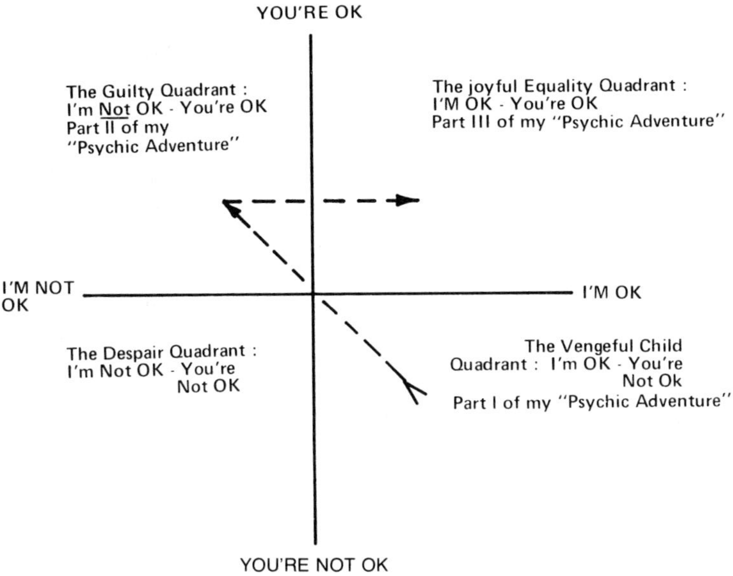

Figure 2—*The "OK Corral" and my voyage therein.*

which Free Child places us and in which we have fun. Alas, it's not common for most of us, whether born there or not, and takes struggle both to attain and to stay in. As bad things happen to us and in the world around, it's not easy to feel the people out in that world are still OK!

Favorite feelings are confidence, love, acceptance, awareness and affirmation.

The fourth black position of *Despair*—I'm Not OK—You're Not OK—is the suicidal one. This can lead to direct suicide or the indirect suicide of alcoholism, drug abuse or accidental death. The favorite feelings are loneliness, unwanted, unloved, cornered, rejected, incapable. At times in TA it's called the *pay-off* position from the fact that being in it gives the equivalent of negative strokes and gives a rich stimulation to the psyche, even though it be despairing. To repeat: we can live on negative strokes; we can't live on no strokes at all!

You will note that I haven't mentioned depression among the

qualities I've listed, as I think it goes with *both* the I'm Not OK positions.

Scripts, Injunctions, Counterscripts and Drivers

Childhood is important because it's in that period, many say within the first seven years, that basic decisions are made which will affect the whole future course of life. The body of these decisions, called a script, is based on what the child assumes the nature of life to be and how she or he can best get along in it.

As with most lives, mine has had both bad and good in it. Many of my script decisions have been extremely hampering or crippling, decisions made because of the painful things that happened to me in childhood as we shall see. Even some of the pleasant things that came led to limiting choices because I easily assumed they were the *only* sources of satisfaction or competence open to me.

Thus, my destiny was formed as it is for most men and women.

Eric Berne's book, *What Do You Say After You Say Hello?* has many fascinating examples of scripts and how they control people's lives, as do other TA books.

The script *injunctions* or commands which are so controlling usually have come early and are not expressed in words by our parents so much as coming deeply and intuitively from their Child to ours. For example, we will see how "Don't Be a Man!" came to me. Attributions—telling us what we are—can be equally controlling as naively in childhood we have no way of questioning these doctrinaire pronouncements. E.g., I was told: "You are awkward; you are shy! You are selfish!"

These negative instructions are often called *Ogre* or *Witch* messages.

By contrast, the opposing *counterscript* comes in the form of words given by Parent, usually Nurturing Parent, as our parents care for us in the form of good worldly aphorisms or advice, which Adaptive Child fastens on as giving it safety in an insecure world. These will probably run counter to the destructive ogre or witch messages of the script and will provide a positive alternate form of behavior to puzzle those who know us. (See Fig. 3.)

An astute young therapist, Taibi Kahler, has pioneered in naming the action of the counterscript through what he calls the "*drivers*" acting in the "*Not-OK miniscript.*" The miniscript is the life script of the person translated or reflected in moment-by-moment action.

These drivers, he maintains, can all be summed up in five specific ones. Though given by well-meaning nurturing parents, and getting their motive power through Adaptive Child, they get us down into the Not-OK position because they generally come from the Not-OK positions of parents and set negative or unattainable goals. The five are as follows:

1. *Please Me.* Please Me is really please the other person. In my case it was "Please Mother" who used to say, "Why can't you do what Mother wants?"
2. *Be Perfect.* Never make a mistake!
3. *Try Hard.* You're bound to fail!
4. *Be Strong.* Don't show the pain or discomfort! Be a man; keep a stiff upper lip!
5. *Hurry Up!*

When we finally decide to live in the I'm OK—You're OK position and be ourselves, free of our limiting script, we can find five opposites of the drivers, as set forth by Hedges Capers, genial counselor and therapist, who calls them the *allowers:*

1. It's OK to please and consider yourself!
2. It's OK to be yourself and make mistakes!
3. You can succeed!
4. Feel and express your feelings—even the painful ones!
5. Take your own time!

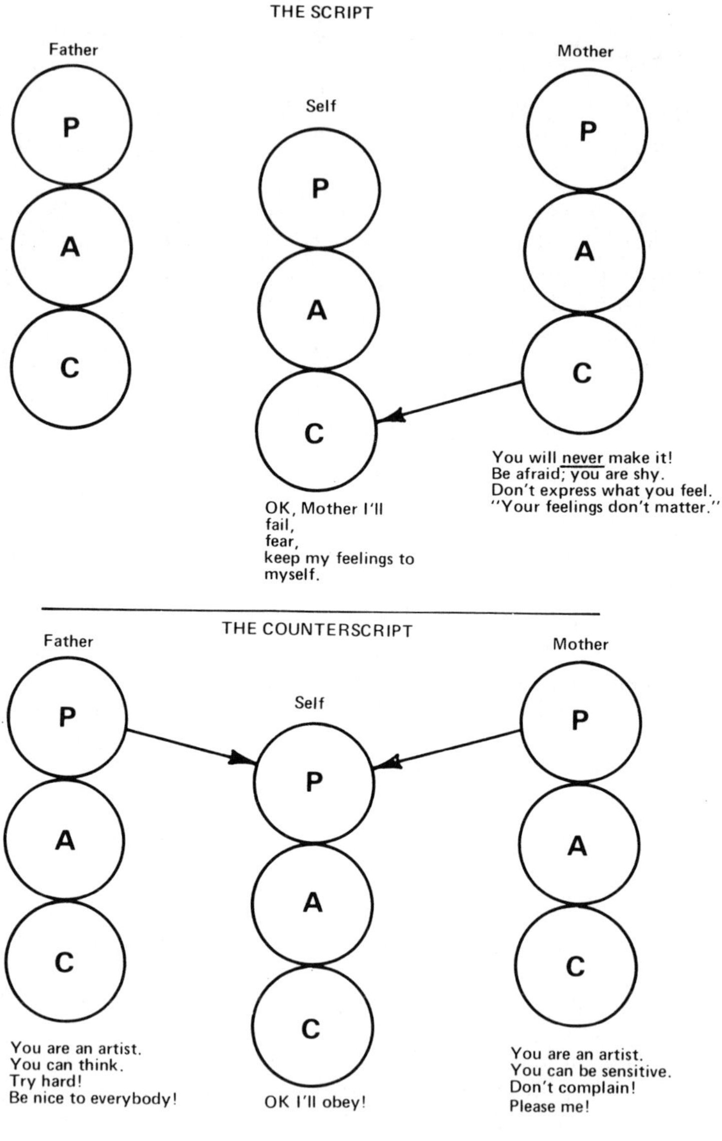
THE SCRIPT
Father
P
A
C
Self
P
A
C
Mother
P
A
C
You will never make it!
Be afraid; you are shy.
Don't express what you feel.
"Your feelings don't matter."
OK, Mother I'll
fail,
fear,
keep my feelings to
myself.
THE COUNTERSCRIPT
Father
P
A
C
Self
P
A
C
Mother
P
A
C
You are an artist.
You can think.
Try hard!
Be nice to everybody!
OK I'll obey!
You are an artist.
You can be sensitive.
Don't complain!
Please me!

Figure 3

Transactions, Games, Payoff

It's clear the stimuli, including the strokes we send out to other people, evoke responses. These exchanges are called *transactions*, which give Transactional Analysis its name.

Many transactions are visible whether involving one ego state or another, whether of a parent scolding a child and getting silence in return, two children playing joyfully together, or a simple request for the time which gets a correct reply.

But many also have hidden parts where the motives involved are not present in the consciousness either of the initiator or the responder. These lead to games, popularized by Eric Berne in his well-known, *Games People Play*. In this study, Berne and TA make specific some of the hitherto uncatalogued maneuvers natural to the behavior of us humans, suspected and used by dramatists and storytellers for centuries but left without name.

As you will find in my story, perhaps my favorite game has been Kick Me, in which my provocative and seemingly Critical-Parent-oriented behavior has been designed to push innocent victims beyond patience to where they will respond with angry vigor. Then my *payoff* will be the desired negative stroke or *kick*. This type of game can be played in miniature but also, as you'll see, in grand design over years. In my life you can finds its beginnings at places like the "Dining Room" table of childhood.

The *Payoff* is the reward to the players of the game in the form of the kind of strokes they have unconsciously sought, reinforcing their favorite positions whether Vengeful, Guilty or Despairing. I believe most Equal strokes are conscious and not gamey.

This brings out the obvious fact that it takes two to play a game. The responder must hook in with the initiator to give what is sought. If the responder is aware, stays in Adult, or simply doesn't care for the reward, there is no game!—For example, in my Kick-Me games, the victims had propensities to revenge which led them to give the desired I'm OK—You're Not OK stroke!

Connections

When I first study a subject, I generally take literally and seriously everything as it's given. In this introduction I've attempted to summarize a lot of the rich TA harvest as it's been presented.

However, as I've used it in my own life and thinking, and in looking at my past life, new connections do pop into my mind not necessarily previously suggested. I offer some herewith.

It seems evident that the basic life positions postulated by Eric Berne relate closely to the ego states he formulates.

To start with the common position: I'm OK—You/He/She/They are Not OK. Clearly the person in whom Vengeful Child is dominant, the result of deprivation or beatings, takes that position as his or her own and lives there. But this person is not the only inhabitant of that quadrant.

The leader type, the aggressive dominating person, also inhabits that quadrant from which he or she can operate calmly as knowing better than the many followers. His or her Vengeful Child may be contained inside his personality, ready to spring out if the will is crossed. But ordinarily it is Controlling Parent that takes the "executive" or commanding role in this person.

Thus Controlling Parent and Vengeful Child take complementary ego states but the same life position. So when in a family or a nation they go hammer and tongs at each other and play games of Uproar or War, they are really close. They understand each other intuitively even if the clash is violent and leads to divorce or death. It's of interest that even those who are fighting to kill each other are playing a mutual game in which each side instinctively perceives and welcomes the hostile moves of the other. Negative strokes of excitement and stimulation are the prizes awarded the game players.

On the other hand, the meek, underdog position: I'm Not OK—You/They are OK is taken by Adaptive Child who can yield either to Controlling Parents or to Vengeful leaders as circumstances dictate. (You might speculate on the Patty Hearst case in that context.) These are the followers in their millions all over the world who make civilizations, organizations, tribes and for whom the leaders compete.

Not that a member of an organization is by any means always a follower in that position. Many union members, for example, are today revolutionaries or rebels on their own who feel more at home in Vengeful Child and by no means do what they are told by their own elected leaders.

The despairing position: I'm Not OK—You/They are Not OK either, may be held by the Adaptive Child when fear penetrates or overwhelms the heart. I'm not as familiar with this position as with the others and there are probably other connections I don't see.

Finally Free Child comes out and welcomes the joyful love position, I'm OK—You're OK, as its own. Adult or the Little Professor may tell it in realistic terms of the faults and dangers inherent in other people. Free Child will agree and act accordingly. But he or she is positive, believes the other person can change, and makes no effort to put him down or punish him. In fact, he or she can enlist his own Adult to help maintain himself or herself in a peaceful state of mind, regardless of outside circumstance. The whole materialist philosophy which relates well-being to material conditions is alien to this smiling Child.

May I give Mother Theresa as an example which may surprise you! Surrounded as she is by people dying and in the worst of conditions, she moves with a flame that springs from the love within. I don't believe that could represent merely a Parent-controlled life: "You should live that way"; or be the result of Adult decisions only: "It's the wisest way for humanity."

To me she demonstrates a Free Child ego state sparked by her Little Professor. In this, her Little Professor, inspired by God if you wish, puts her at immediate grips with a world need and yet maintains within her a fountain of joy.

Not all of us are called to do what she does; that would be imitation in Adaptive Child. We may, however, be called to live: I'm OK—You're OK, and do the thing that is unique for us.

But enough of formuli and abstract conceptions! Let us get into my life in which all these things come into play!

Preface

All of the people you will read about are real. They *lived.* Many still live.

But as I have lived, I have seen them as through colored glasses. I have seen them through the fiery, passionate eyes of a little boy, of a disturbed adolescent, of a hating young man, and so on, of myself. Remember that is prejudice—that is not neutral.

So may they not be offended for themselves!—They may not even recognize themselves as they wouldn't in a bad photo. May they not be offended for each other, but only, if at all, with me the author!

PART I

I'LL SHOW YOU I WILL!

CHAPTER ONE

Childhood

The Big House

I was born in a big house as one of a big family. It was a huge, well-built palace of a house with many windows through which poured the sun. It stood by itself on a gentle hill with neighbors respectfully some yards away. Far off on either side where came up the sun and set the sun were two mighty cliffs of stone, known to all who love New Haven as East Rock and West Rock, respectively. There was space; there was quantity; there was adventure.

I was never to feel totally blocked or shut in. Certainly the fourth or suicidal basic life position: I'm Not OK—You're Not OK—Nothing's OK has never appealed to me.

Naturally such a big house required many people to maintain it in the standards of those days, the nineteen-tens. There were nurses, governesses, maids, a cook, a laundress, a chauffeur and a wonderful black man named Joseph who supervised the building and grounds. He had a vast cellar as his domain, full of bins and coal. Most of these people were kindly and gave good strokes to a wide-eyed boy.

There was a tale I heard of a "bad" miss, who had spanked me unmercifully and been fired, but memory doesn't give anything specific that isn't merged with the gigantic figures of the two commanding presences of the household: Mother and Father.

Mother

As a mother with a babe in arms, Mother was a beautiful woman. The babe's dependency brought out all the nurturing love that I believe is latent in all men and women.

She enjoyed this symbiosis so much that she never wanted to relinquish it. She was a little woman with a rather long, oval face. She fantasized endlessly, almost brooded, with her mouth drawn into a Mona Lisa smile which later became fixed. I knew it well as I gazed at it, fascinated, in spite of my rebellion.

The smile continued what the words had said: Mother knows best. And indeed, when I am a dependent baby, mother does know best.

Positive strokes in her own childhood had been very conditional: You Can Be OK If . . . negative strokes were multiple and certain with every infraction, though I imagine in her "gentle" cultured home a blow was rare; the word was the instrument of power. Father had been an unchallenged god.

She was drawn to her father and I guess she felt she understood his shyness better than her outgoing mother who loved to see and care for and organize people in numbers. Some of the fantasy may have involved going away with the loved one to a place where the two could have deep platonic intimacy of souls.

As we've seen, the Adaptive Child is the part of Child that induces learning of the rules imposed by parent figures in order better to survive with them and earn their strokes. Mother, since in the manner of most Victorian households good strokes were conditional on good behaviour, was encouraged to build a life on good-behaviour rules. Thus, in effect, like millions of other humans, she enthroned Parent and its content of instructions as ultimate authority and source of much satisfaction.

The Adaptive Child is fearful. And I believe if it and its counterpart, Controlling Parent (Steiner lumps them all under one head as "Pig Parent"!), are given the right and power, fear is installed alongside.

This explains where her fear and also mine came from as I chose the same power inside. For a great fear communicated itself to me.

She wouldn't speak of the fear, which I could read mostly in her eyes as the pupils dilated. For right was in Parent and as long as its authority was maintained, all would have to be well.

Though I chose fear, for forty years I was not to choose the rules except overtly. What happened with my fear and my rebellion will be a large part of this story as it unfolds.

Mother's father, Alfred Mitchell, had wanted a man child. Her name of Alfreda reflects this wish. She was given a difficult script injunction: Don't Be You—Be a Man. Thus, she had to maintain the authority supposedly associated with that sex. Marriage brought her seven sons. I was number six and by that time she longed for a daughter. We shall see what message was transmitted to me.

However, for those early years of dependent infanthood I was in a paradise of love in which her lovely care predominated.

It's No Use Crying—Go to Sleep!

I suppose I was suckled mainly on a bottle—and more certainly on a schedule. There was a central nursery room or the room next to Mother's where the babies were kept.

My next thoughts are deductions. I have no direct evidence of my own memories or those of my older brothers to support the theory, but a sense that this is exactly what would be done.

The Parent doctrine that if you give in to a child, he or she will get "spoiled" was strongly held. Once a schedule or routine was decided on, it had to be maintained come hell or high water, otherwise Parent would lose her authority and the child would suffer the intolerable damage of getting his own way.

My postulate is that when I cried, unless it was bottle time or exercise time or change-the-diapers time, I was left to cry myself to sleep—that would be normal.

Much later in the days of marriage, especially when my wife, Norris, and I went out together or to a show, and I wasn't getting the recognition I wanted, the strokes I needed, I would go to sleep. Others would ignore it embarrassedly; I would fight it fruitlessly—not knowing the cause.

It seems the baby that I had been must have long ago decided in the depths of my inmost being: *It's no use crying: go to sleep!* So still when I feel I'm being ignored, I'll bypass making a forbidden noise and suddenly wake up with a jolt and a stiff neck—the show is over; it's time to go home.

Mother's Room and the Library

Mother's room was a big, comfortable one with a high wingbacked armchair in a big parrot pattern and cosy cushions. On the walls were reproductions of Italian madonnas, Botticelli, Rafael, as well as small landscapes bought through the years at the Lyme Art Gallery. Corot loomed mistily in sepia.

The beds were luxurious. I suppose I was born in one. The earliest memories are of the room as joyous, and babyhood as a Golden Age, which came to an end with the arrival of the youngest brother, Jonathan, or Jack as we called him.

I believe the madonnas are revealing of her character as is the Mona Lisa smile. Sex was a no-no, but motherhood was glorious and most deserving of good strokes, so she had to endure and become a mother. The Virgin was the ideal who conceived without a man.

Whether deeper down, hidden in the recesses of Child, she liked sex after all, I'm not competent to say. That must remain her secret with her Maker.

I don't think of it as Father's room, although the big tub in the bathroom, the mysterious shaving tools, were for him. His presence was much more down the steep little extra stairway to the library below. Every wall was laden with books from floor to ceiling, even weighing down one or two "secret" doors. There were a huge desk, a revolving bookcase and vast leather armchairs before the fire. There, too, were a green-shaded lamp, and a Holbein print which folded out in front of the books.

He liked to read to us and, in truth, it was good, curled up in that generous arm to listen to his dramatic rendition of Oliver Herford's "Earthquake" or Kipling's "Bell" boom out: "Not he!"

The Explorer

Father was a tall, handsome man, broad of face with a commanding forehead and a luxuriant shock of straight white hair.

To his first sons he had given lots of time and attention. But he was busy with a demanding varied career and by the time I came along couldn't give much time to parenthood. However, Nurturing Parent came on strong and the desire to get close to each one, though he didn't always seem to know how. When he was in Critical Parent, he gave it free and formidable rein, which frightened me as well as others of us.

The reader will see that he gave me lots of encouraging positive strokes and that each bore rich fruit in the areas thus chosen. However, there were few unconditional strokes, the loving acceptance as is, which meant so much from Granny and others of the lower orders in the household. The result was that I could never quite relax with him as truly myself and not as achiever.

The key to his life is as explorer. The explorer not only finds, investigates, taps and uses resources, proclaims to the world his joyful new thing. He also eventually looks around, breaks away and goes on with some effort and pain to the next territory, no matter how fruitful and rewarding the last one has been.

Father gave me in this a model for which I am fervently grateful. He was an early example of a man not content with one career, no matter how successful. Far from resting on his laurels with the famous archeological find of Machu Picchu, above the torrents of the Urubamba, he went on to the even more hazardous and shoal-ridden river of U.S. politics where, after some brilliant conquests, he crashed on the hard rock of defeat and neglect and remained there for many years.

> . . . yet all experience is an arch wherethrough
> Gleams that untravelled world, whose margin fades
> For ever and for ever when I move.

I was to follow that same path in the realms of the imagination or mind.

Fratricide—Patricide—Seven Brothers

Whether or how much all families are symbiotic I don't know. Aaron and Jacqui Schiff (in the *ITAA Journal,* Vol. 1, No. 1, "Passivity") discuss how in what they call a "symbiotic family" the talents are divided up "with no reference to external reality, and with all characteristics identified as extreme, i.e., Johnny and Jimmy may have similar intelligence, but Jimmy is defined as intelligent and Johnny as outgoing or artistic. In this situation Johnny is scripted not to achieve academically (to do so would be fratricide) and Jimmy may not have friends or be creative."

This may well grow out of the jealousy and competition for the mother's or father's love so well brought out in the Freudian approach.

In our large family it was certainly that way. The attributions thus symbiotically given stuck as fundamental formative parts of our scripts. For example, I was told I was the "artist" of the family. This not only formed me with its encouragement; it discouraged the others who might have been equally gifted. For them it would have been fratricide to take up art.

Perhaps fratricide is too strong a word. But it well suggests the strength of the prohibition *against* competing with a sister or brother in her or his "given" field. As we shall see, these prohibitions affected me in various ways both in sports and in scholarship.

I've mentioned how Father was my model in exploring. This was not patricidal because it was in a different field.

I don't want to mention each brother separately now. They will pop up individually in due course. But it's interesting that of the two in the same sphere as his, that of politics, one has been *unsuccessful,* thus providing no patricidal parallelism, and the other so far is in Congress as a representative but not a senator as he was.

This kind of family is in obvious contrast to one where junior specifically follows in father's footsteps. I suspect the competitive factor is weaker there and they live more in the "I'm OK—You're OK" life position than we did.

Is there anything I can say about the seven brothers as a whole?

Culturally Mother told us: "You are better than anybody else. The Bingham brothers are superior. We're OK—They are Not OK!"

Childhood and Vengeful Child

Of childhood I'll omit many details. I don't need to go over all the good and pleasant things we did. All the play. There was plenty of it. But the color of childhood wasn't all bright. We trembled under the counterscript: "You Can Be OK If . . . " I never knew when the "monstrous black crow" would come, the crow of punishment "You are *Not* OK!"

There is a part of Child which reacts. If violence is done, either physical or even violence in not giving the person enough strokes, I'm sure the mind can easily take the position: I'm OK—You're Not OK. This part is called Vengeful or Rebellious Child. From this spring the hostile and aggressive forces that can govern throughout life.

But the power of Vengeful Child is limited, destructive though it may be in intent. It cannot survive by attacking the powerful parents who may have originally caused the pain. For they control its ability to survive at all and to receive strokes. Neither does it directly attack Parent which has been installed as a monitoring voice inside the head.

It may even seek an alliance with Parent by showing other harmful things in the outside world and together they can voice an: "Ain't It Awful" or beyond that: "Let's Get *Them;* Let's Kill *Them!*"

Hundreds of times I imagined as a child that I had a magic talisman, the *Wishing Ring*—especially when going off to sleep—which would bestow all the prestige and potency I wanted but of which the outside world was depriving me. However, specific action in these fantasies was limited to providing munificent presents for the loved ones, for example a clock surrounded by many columns for Mother.

Whereas, the negative action sought by my own Vengeful Child could get through into consciousness and gain the approval of Parent only by confining itself to those further away, to *Them.* The world was at war (1914-1918). I drew pictures defeating Germans or shot them down in tin-soldier form!

As we shall see, I was faced in my childhood with a negative script which consisted of a series of negative commands or injunctions and attributes which told me what I am: Don't Be You; You Will *Never* Attain; You Are Shy; You Are Awkward; You Are Slow, and so on. The negative part inside me, seat of Vengeful Child, wouldn't accept such commands without reacting. So its basic thesis for the first forty years of my life became: "I can and will attain! I'll show you I will!" This determination would be unconscious but corrupt every action. For example, the marriage bed was troubled by it, as we shall see. Nothing could henceforth be simple pleasure—which Parent frowned on. It would have to have the impure implication: "You see—I told you I could!"

Sex

Sex had its dark side and its light side—localized for me in bathrooms, one at each end of the great house.

The tiny nursery bathroom was about the only place where it was OK to be naked—except later at the old swimmin' hole in Salem, way down the brook. All the delights of feeling skin, tingling in the warmth of the hot bath—oceans deep—with a warm, loving lady soaping and holding a towel and enmeshed herself in the conspiracy of good feelings!

Once or twice, greatly daring, I would urinate into the bath, violating all the codes so strictly built up around that function, somehow aware that her chiding would be so mild, interlarded perhaps with a chuckle, that it would only enhance the freedom I felt. I was shocked disapprovingly, however, if younger brother Jack did it.

Mother's bathroom was huge, with two basins, an extra-length tub planted in the middle. It might be all right to peek in there—if given permission, to appreciate the elegance of special square bottles with names on them to hold perfumes and toiletries. But that was where every few months—or so it seemed—a horror ceremony was enacted.

Castration

The doctor, whom we called Dr. Calomel from his fondness for that prescription, ordinarily a merry soul with an unforgettable high-pitched laugh which he exploded after each one of his stories, so that the child was far more fascinated by the laugh than by the words, was the principal active agent in the drama. The ceremony, I have learned since, was for retraction of the foreskin to avoid future constriction—"It's all for your good." But the most important participant as far as the message conveyed to me was concerned, was Mother.

Stripped—with that frail organ, the penis, exposed to pain and indignity, Dr. Calomel's face wrinkled in distaste—with Mother hovering in the background, the strongest feeling came through of her enjoyment and thrill in what was taking place. *You will never be a man,* was the message I acquired, however far that was from the conscious minds of the others. A nightmare, due to be repeated and repeated and thus never put behind.

You are Not OK! We, the powerful ones, are OK and know best for you!

This central scene of my childhood more than any other helps to explain and add poignancy to the difficult years of marriage that were to come, the turning away into a sexless organization, and finally the liberation through T.A.—it's OK to be a man!

And with Hilda, to whom I've joined my life most recently, the reincarnation in the present of the loving women in the nursery, I've been able to find a wholly-free acceptance of manhood and womanhood, where faith replaces no-no, and I'm no longer castrated!

The Red Queen

When a man child is not wanted, when the mother would have preferred a girl, the idea gets across whether she ever says it aloud or not. Don't be You—Be something else.

Eric Berne suggests that the strength of mythology and the fairy tale is that in making our script decisions we are helped by the example or patterns these stories give us. We choose mythical heroes or heroines which magically exemplify the characteristics we have chosen for ourselves. Examples can be Hercules or Jason or Superman, Cleopatra, Juno, Florence Nightingale or Billie Jean King.

I believe that the person I thus chose was Alice, the dreamy heroine with long hair of *Alice Through the Looking Glass*. This was one of my favorite books. Alice, in a world where everything was reversed, i.e., boys could be girls, went passively through many encounters unable to effect the course of her adventures but still the heroine, who is the focus of attention.

The most potent figure that emerges in that story is the Red Queen, the no-no phantasm who knows best and puts Alice down with all the severity of Critical Parent. This superficially distorting picture of Mother gives a deeply real view of how she appeared to me. Alice is never exactly thrilled by the negative strokes she gets but she does get them.

The White Queen, on the other hand, represents a Nurturing Parent who has no power and fades back and forth into a sheep or a harried fugitive from time.

Back of Alice in my life is the more shadowy universal figure of Tantalus, symbolizing that my wants can *never* be fulfilled.

What can a boy do whose instructions are not to be himself? Or who is told that he can *never* attain? Dream, yes. But also decide revengefully that he can. I'll show you that I can be a man, a hero, a Velasquez; I can marry, have children and enjoy the delights of touch.

He doesn't know, poor devil, that that is still being controlled by the Red Queen! That he is not free. Rebelling is always rebelling *against* something and requires the You-are-Not-OKness of the other.

Years later, my friends in the movement I was in, called Moral Re-Armament, used to tell me that when I reacted still—in my forties as a supposedly mature man to Mother's dominating instruction—I was controlled by my rebellion. Neither they nor I knew that what was needed was a simple permission *not* to be that way—a permission in some such words as these: "The early decision you made is out of date. You *are* free now. It's no longer—I'll show you; but yes, go ahead and do it without relation to Parent at all."

My beautiful loving mother herself was neither malicious nor aware of the effect of her Parent ego state on the sensitive plasticity of the life she had borne, and of her Parent saying: "That's the way it must be!"

Only now can I and the rest of us humans, through the illumination that has come, get unshackled from the bonds of script and mold our lives to suit the more genial lifestyle and love that emanate from Free Child!

Dry Sex

What I described before as good, warm life-giving was the wet sex of the tub.

There was also a less conscious reaction that found me often as a small boy reaching for my pants and tweaking the little phallus or testicles within. Somehow this action rarely failed to attract the supervisory eye of Mother.

I would awaken to what I was doing with the prohibition: "Don't touch yourself" already reaching my ears. It seems there was a tiny dry itch which sought a scratch through the subconscious.

Little Professor might whisper to me: "Scratching is OK if you don't do it so often as to catch Mother's eye." But, goaded by the desire to please her, whom I loved and from whom came the strokes I wanted, I was already learning without verbal elaboration from her the following commands: "Those parts are forbidden—we don't talk about them—we can't enjoy them—we skip over them when we're drying or feeling our muscles from top to bottom or bottom to top."

Little Professor soon realizes that sex is forbidden, except in certain areas or certain hidden circumstances. It is a puzzling taboo because pleasure can result, but the world, at least my world, won't allow it.

Thus I was building up a powerful inhibiting force in my psyche which would from Parent act to smother or deflect the natural urges which flow from Free Child. Adaptive Child, the "Spooky" part which wants to please the holders of power and the controllers of strokes, thus betrays the other parts of Child, Free Natural Child, with a permanent restraint. Only much later with understanding can a quasimiraculous deliverance free the crippled Eros.

Permission

Thinking back, I am amazed at how I picked up in the middle of countless no-nos, a permission to observe, to think, to see as long as I kept all that to myself. All the punishments or worse, the putdowns by older brothers eager to display their superiority in the pecking order and nearness to authority, involved what was said! No wonder I made a profound decision to go on thinking—I'm OK—They are Not—but *to say nothing*. Conformity in words; my mind is free. Thus the sweatshirt message, which was put into words at one of my first schools as we shall hear, of "*Living Statue*" on the front, and hidden on the back: "To Hell With You!"

I still do it. On the New York subway, for example, where virtually no one has permission to look, my looks go from face to face of that fascinating array and read thousands of lives displayed in all their mystery and wonder. And now—Thank God!—due to TA, I no longer think "What's wrong with you?" I can see them as OK.

Art

The great house overflowed with culture. It's a wonder that that ploy wasn't seized on before I came along to claim it. However, the Don't-Be-You message must have been getting stronger as more and more boys appeared and disavowed her desire for a daughter. Culture was Mother's prerogative. And the older boys may have taken more of a model after Father, the man.

When I was ten, Father gave me an adult illustrated book on Velasquez. I loved this as I earlier loved the stuffed giraffe he had given me when I was ill. The book flattered the growing Adult inside—you can be grown up in this area at least. I pored over the reproductions, especially Philip himself, self-satisfied and OK, the "Surrender of Breda," compassion in the midst of arrogance, "Christ at the Column," the child could give a drop of comfort to the fallen Lord. All in all a rich and somber scene.

Alas, I have preserved no childhood drawings! The puritan art ethic—*it must look like what it is*—was still too strong to have permitted saving such formless endeavors. "Childish scribble" were still putdown words at that time.

My earliest clear memories of the direction my destiny was taking are of undertaking a series of precise drawings in pencil of the Parthenon frieze, of which we had many large casts ornamenting the living room. Horses and riders in gracious confusion, one after another, were appropriately and almost impossibly difficult to reproduce, thus provoking many positive strokes of encouragement. I believe the drawings were fair. To this day I retain a grateful love for the medium, pencil, though bold ink passed it in favor of use much later.

At Groton—to jump for a moment into adolescence—I was introduced to charcoal, a messy, laborious tool which in retrospect seems designed to kill the budding creativity. I was made to understand that it was a necessary learning medium. Grimy, dusty, I sweated and labored long over drawing the Michelangelo casts—shading and scraping.

Kleber Hall, a slow-spoken art teacher whom, recalling, I suspect of bitterness, was grudging in strokes and demanded it be done his way—the first of an immeasurably long line of art teachers of whom that can be said. Yet he put my large creations up in the public halls, and I, who could gather no strokes in popularity or sports, few in studies, took what comfort I could from this recognition—confirming that here, at least, was a field in which I could be somebody.

Though I wouldn't touch charcoal now—my fingers shrink from the mere thought, I do love Michelangelo as I love the Greeks.

One epic struggle occurred with Kleber. I had somehow branched into ink—I suppose I am forever branching—and had undertaken a water scene, with some pilings and swirling reflections. This may have been closer to his field of illustration. In any case, I was required to do those damned reflections over and over till I was incredibly nauseated with the whole project.

Color Blossoms

Sometime in the early days of one of those long summers which blissfully dragged on between the hells of Form X and Form Y, I was given a course of lessons in oil painting with a gentle Yankee named Gregory Smith in the neighboring village of Old Lyme. I remember best the first time I went, after being outfitted with easel, brushes, some tubes of color and some boards on which to practice. He stuck me out in the middle of the field back of his house, arching towards trees and a house or two in the distance, and said, "Paint!" I was launched into what quickly became ecstasy.

Once or twice during the course of the long afternoon he would wander out to where I was working and offer some criticism. Lyme was in the throes of an Americanization of the work of the Impressionists. Greg Smith, who turned out low key "Nocturnes" himself, had the grace to let me learn from the sun and air and color that God Himself had put into New England.

I soon worked every day and not just lesson days. For all those glorious hours I forgot Mitch—Living Statue and all—and became absorbed in nature. This became a passion that carried through all the remaining years of purgatory and remained a constant in young manhood when all else seemed to fail.

Only a more powerful force was fated to interrupt what seemed the only positive satisfaction always available. I not only could get good strokes from others for what I did, but learned to give myself good strokes for work done.

Ruskin

In his way of giving a big push with a few words, Father had showed me on the shelves and recommended a five volume set of Ruskin's *Modern Painters* as being of value for one who was interested. Not daunted by the length—for me a long book promised more—and perhaps enticed by all the fascinating illustrations, I plunged in and was soon captured.

For those who haven't experienced his sonorous prose, his passionate enthusiasm or the real care with which he tackles aspects of nature—a whole long section on rocks, on trees, on mountains, on clouds—I can only say John Ruskin bound me permanently through all the rebellious upset of Cubism and its derivatives to observation and love of all that I see around me. He has given me a lifetime of enrichment.

A Class Society

I can't, of course, speak for those who've come from less privileged classes; I can only infer. But I have a hunch that the origin of class differences and the class war start in the home.

At the top obviously are the leaders, Father and Mother. Our father was away a lot, busy with his career of exploration. That gave her the *power!*

Then there is the middle class composed of brothers, sisters, aunts, uncles and all the other grown-ups around.

The older brothers—I had no sisters—who ranked higher

than I, were perhaps fairly insecure themselves but in any case wanted much of the time to establish their position in the "pecking order." So any infringement of the rules was pounced upon by eagle eyes. As we'll see in a few pages, this was especially strong at the dining room table.

Along with these in the "middle" classes might be ranked all the various people who worked in the home. Most of them were amazingly nurturing souls who would always give a stroke to one who needed it. Smith, the chauffeur, gave me rides to school on the coldest days, when bicycles would be cruel, tucking a warm laprobe around my knees. It was clear that here was a steady love that I could count on. It was the same with Joseph, the black with a mottled face—he had had head injuries—whose care was constant.

The lower class—the powerless one—unlike society itself, where the majority are in the lowest ranks, was one person, little I. I had no power over others. I was resentful and afraid to express the resentment. Mother had said, *"Your feelings don't matter!"*

With all the different horrible struggles that divide mankind based on differences of religion, class or race, is it not possible that the fire and fury with which we pursue these struggles derive their vigor from our Child-held resentment against *them,* against those who had the power when we were small and felt powerless? If this be so and we can be brought to see it, to move from Vengeful Child to a new position, then there is hope that we can find an answer in Adult to the issues that arise between us.

I believe our predisposition, our desire is to blame and take action involving negative strokes of excitement and harm. Some of us, however, clear now on the scripty origin of anger, can demonstrate reliance on positive strokes and understanding which will lead others to find the same. I'm OK—You're OK can be contagious.

Granted that conditions in the world are terribly unequal and need to be changed. Granted that possessors, that dominating races and various other combinations of humans have done wrong throughout history in oppressing others. A positive attitude in us can bring answers to these things more quickly and permanently than a vengeful negativism which gets us into games. I believe as we get free of harmful scripting we will find ourselves healing these very situations.

Granny

It gradually became apparent that there was another person in the "upper class," my mother's mother, known to us as Granny. Mother had a deferential love for her that was different. The respect communicated itself and I knew she was special.

A tiny woman, recently widowed, by the time I remember her, she was always dressed in lacy, dainty white with a Queen Victoria cap on her head. Rather than being regal, she emanated grace.

With me she was always loving, nurturing, "fond," as she liked to call it. She could sharply define the areas of good behavior and bad behavior, but this never bothered one bit, as it was secure that I was OK and loved!

I loved her rambling house in New London, with all the stairs, wide porches, infinite lawns stretching away, picture windows that let in all the summer air. An elegant black butler named Tully served a unique fruit punch. At meals we sat on little chairs and looked at round box bushes outside. Once in a while, to mark a ceremonial occasion, a dusty bottle of claret would come out of the cellar—left over from Grandfather's day. We might have a sip. The memory of this taste is far removed in kind from anything experienced in more than fifty years since.

Part of the spacious expanse of the property was a slope down to Pequot Avenue, which passed in front outside a massive gate and wall, and beyond that more land, a beach and the harbor with its many ships. It was up this slope that the house had grown in stages of enlargement from a fisherman's prim cottage to the Frank Lloyd Wright-like generosity of the final stage. This accounted for the fascination of the big and little, front and back, top and bottom stairs which led magically from one part to another and around without backtracking.

Equally active on the slope outside we would get into the bottom half of her round wicker chairs and roll down in ecstatic abandon.

Farther off in the back was a giant collection of flowers, fruits and vegetables presided over by Gustave, the gardener brought over from Germany. Still further beyond more walls was a woods where sailed a great smooth rock on which we could pass right to Fairyland or get marooned on a desert island.

Granny was a unique member of the "Upper Class" and appears in my life as the beneficent fairy-godmother.

Training

Sometimes I wonder whether if you have to have a brother or sister born after you, it were better to have the replacement come within two years so memory will hardly know any other state, or later when Adult is somewhat developed and can cope with the conditions that all is changed, that I am no longer the favored, nurtured baby who is closest to Mother's breast.

In any case, I could know nothing at that time of such choices. In April of 1914, when I was almost three and one-half, the blow fell. Suddenly the golden age was over.

I awake to myself as a person with strong negative strokes coming because I am failing to learn the bowel and bladder control necessary to OKness in my world, or am slipping back from what I've already learned.

It seems the bed, when I wake up in the morning, is Not-OK. Usually wet. Sometimes with unpleasant BMs in it, too. Vigorous spankings result. I think of Father's power expressing itself in no uncertain terms that I am bad and must learn better.

This hell couldn't have lasted long—probably I did change fairly soon.

However, the victory was not complete. Vengeful Child, aroused as in all humans by negative strokes, by injunctions that: You are Not OK, had many tricks with which to express revolt and trip up the child who suffered and was forced to get existential satisfaction out of that suffering.

Not only must the civilized child that I was expected to become relinquish the pleasure of "going" to the bathroom when he pleases, he must perform faithfully once a day at the required time, in our case after breakfast. But, alas, buried deep in the cortex was the revolt. I might sit on the toilet at that time, sit if need be for half an hour or an hour, forced into that action by powers stronger than I, but no material was necessarily forthcoming.

Burned into my Critical Parent was the injunction: Do Not Lie—Tell the Truth. But under the weight of those dead sitting spells, for me who wanted to get out and play at any of the various games, in or out, that were waiting, I learned to lie. If I said that I had "gone," had dutifully flushed the toilet, the powers that be seemed satisfied and let me get away with it.

I never forgot those lies!

Subsequently we will see what happened when years later I tried to put that right with my Father and got grievously misunderstood.

Wetting the pants at times of excitement or stress lasted longer and thus was a more painful problem. Father would say: "Plan, plan ahead—then you'll get through." And when I felt OK, I'm sure this would happen. But Vengeful Child and the taste for negative excitement were stronger than the conscious will and betrayed me into another trauma each time.

This happened often and I will give an example not from early childhood but from, say, the ten-year-old stage.

Early I loved the piano; we had a beautiful player piano, the Welte Mignon, which reproduced among many: Beethoven's sonatas rendered by Paderewski, Chopin, and a special favorite, Schubert's "Erlking." As children, Jack and I used to dance around in free rhythm to it. So when an aging, kindly spinster, our Cousin Kate, offered to teach me to play, I was thrilled. This went on for a while.

However, Mother, who was a talented violinist and *knew*

best about music, wanted to make a little chamber orchestra of her family. Alfred and Brewster already played the piano—she was tired of the "Erlking." So it was decreed that I would switch to the clarinet, an instrument of "beautiful tone." One was duly purchased and I was sent to New London from Salem to take lessons with a homely but skillful Jew named Feltcorn. I'm sure the gentleman was agreeable and pleasant. But I had not been consulted, my feelings were ignored—"They don't matter," and I hated the compulsory changeover to something that was complex and difficult to learn.

So every time, every lesson—I was far too shy to ask for the bathroom—I would end up with a telltale stain on the trousers and have to retreat to Salem in agony. Mr. Feltcorn never seemed to see. How often this actually happened, I don't know, but as with so many childhood shocks, there seems no limit.

Jealousy

All this might not have happened or been so severe if the younger sibling had not arrived just when he did, i.e., when I had reached the crucial toilet training stage. Of course at the time I had no idea of any connection between my difficulties remaining continent and the inordinate jealousy that I suddenly found gripping my feelings.

Jack was an agreeable boy—he had a freedom with others but felt put down by his brothers with all their rules learned so faithfully in Adaptive Child. But I could see no good in him—except during an occasional scamper. Love thy neighbor; love thy brother, were not yet in my vocabulary. And since I had decided to suppress feelings, not to express felt emotions, I suppose I had no difficulty in hiding this.

Why, oh why, were there no wise eyes examining me and caring enough to guess my secrets, no understanding heart to smooth the crises of boyhood? So much care was given to nurture the body, so so little to nourish the soul!

One incident stands out.

Dressed in the "woolies" with which the attentive powers had enveloped us one wintry day, Jack and I were outside to play. Perhaps the usual pursuits were flagging—there was no snow which gave endless entertainment in those years.

Pushed by some demon of opportunity, I announced that one particular little evergreen was mine and no one was allowed to touch it or infringe thereon. Admittedly it was a game, as I knew it wasn't really mine, but a deadly serious game withal. Of course, no self respecting brother whose Spunky Child was ever to the fore, could refrain from picking up the gauntlet thus thrown down. He plucked a twig from the sacred tree.

Aflame with righteous indignation, the rules of good conduct pushed aside, I attacked. As a smaller person he fled and I pursued.

Into the house. Somehow into the back hall, where he went down, I on top. Cries of alarm rent the air.

Parents were out but the good Cousin Kate came along. Her solution was to scold and separate us both. I explained the provocation and was dismayed that somehow it failed to absolve me from fault. Among brothers the doctrine of "Fair Warning" had served to justify various mayhems. This didn't seem to extend to an adult member of the household.

Entirely apart from the ethics of who-is-to-blame, which never get anywhere in a legal way, I believe this little encounter epitomizes the hostility that was ever ready to spring to the fore in my jealous spirit. Provocation grows out of a vengeful desire and then closes its eyes to its own part—I'm OK—He's Not OK.

Nursery

There was a big room in the center of the second floor which was designated as a nursery where a child would be before he became enough of a specific individual to have a room of his own or at least have a governess to teach him things. In the nursery he would have a nurse to see to his creature comforts and help him through the "training" period on to the "learning" period. It was all on a schedule.

Fortunately the words "nurse" and "nursery" come from the same roots as "nourish"—to suckle. These generous-hearted women who gave of their love and affection without hope of permanent return and without the power and position of Mother, helped the child, sensitive as a mimosa, to survive and grow. In mind, in dreams he could always return to this care as to the ocean, the womb.

As I mentioned, there did seem to have been one who was censorious. The word "stupid" on which I'll comment shortly, may have had its roots here. But that, like a bad fairy tale, lives mostly as something I was told about; any actual trauma, memory has not preserved.

There I learned to eat, to play, to be sick. Play soon expanded to include the whole house when the omens were favorable—living room, out-of-doors, gymnasium, even library when Father was not at home if we were careful.

But eating with a bib—there could be no survival without a bib with its two strings—was at first confined to that upstairs room. There may have been foods I didn't like—there were certainly things like strawberries that I did. The atmosphere was fun and protected. I had a chance to protest, even to be naughty without jeopardizing the fundamental generosity with which I was nurtured.

Dining Room

Alas, one has to grow up! Spunky, never having been too much encouraged, I was reluctant to take each new step. Spooky, Adaptive Child, always shouted loudly of the dangers ahead; a fertile imagination can play into Spooky's game.

But needs must when the heavyweights decide. It was time I ate in the dining room with the rest of the family. I had no contrapower with which to resist. There were probably elements within myself that wanted me to go on—though hidden, Spunky must have existed.

Once again I awake—this time to a rigid social structure where there is much suitable behaviour to learn, called by the dread name of "Table Manners." Adaptive Child gets busy; Rebellious Child waits in the wings preparing revenge.

At each end of the beautiful, shiny mahogany table with the spreading lion's-paw legs (I have it still!) sat the powers-that-be. I faced the windows with my back to the lovely Portuguese-tiled fireplace and looked out on the terrace and the lawn with Father on the right and Mother to the left. Between were ranked the older brothers, with me somewhere in the middle.

The hierarchy was clear. Father liked to talk and talked well. Many stories were told. We listened. The French governess, Mlle. Léonie Bernard, whom we called "Mademoiselle," was often there. Then the conversation shifted to French. Anyone using an English word was subject to fine—after we had reached the age of allowances.

But Father was often away. Mother gave responsibility to the "older" ones. Just as strictly as ever, hierarchy was adhered to. If I said anything out of my uncertain knowledge of the world, I would usually be told in no uncertain terms that that was a "dumb" or "stupid" remark.

To this day I find myself excoriating myself with a "stupid" with virtual pleasure after any little mistake—like a throwback to those far-off times!

Lest you think the decision not to talk, to be a "living statue" as I was later called, came natural, that I am built that way through genes, I must relate that at other times when Jack and I or Bruce and I were alone with a kindly nurse, I would chatter like any house finch, of whom there were hundreds who came to caucus in our wisteria on the second-floor balcony. At other moments I would pester with questions or whine if I wanted something that was not forthcoming. No, it was a crippling script decision limiting the talk that was as natural to me as to any human. So that I couldn't be free with groups.

Years later when I was working, as we shall see, in a group dedicated to saving humanity called "Moral Re-Armament" and our family home in Miami was used for that purpose with many young and older people staying there who were giving all their time to it, we ate all our meals together. These were graciously prepared and graciously served and talk would sparkle around the long table.

But I would think in fury: "Why don't they ever let me get a word in?" It took much help of a friend like Jim Newton to get me to see that I was holding back, living once again in the state of rage of I'm OK—They're Not OK, which had become so familiar.

Somehow it was around this key, this classic situation of childhood that awkwardness developed also. As with so many bad, repetitive things I don't remember the first time. But I find myself spilling the water which was placed in a delicate glass on the right, at almost every single meal. I believe negative strokes—a loud "You're clumsy"—showed my young self that here was a sure-fire way to gain regard after the neglect and reduction to silence. Negative strokes are more life-giving than no strokes at all, and I early became addicted to them.

In Parent we say casually: "Oh, he (or she) just wants attention." There is profound truth in that, but also a vicious implication that wanting attention is wrong! We all want it, need it, and woe betide us if we don't give it to each other!

It got so bad they put a special napkin in front of my place each day to hold the flood. And that napkin has remained in my mind like a flag of honor, an indication of my specialness.

The spilling was a silent revenge, a discomfort-creating act which yet captured notice. I felt badly over the "Clumsy!" or "There he goes again," with which it was greeted, but got strokes of concern and negative care out of it. Thus I could be victim who resents all his punishers and punishment, and get a payoff of I'm OK (I couldn't help it)—They're Not OK (They're mean!). It was a situation I thought I didn't want, yet I sought it again and again. The Kick-Me game was developing early.

The Schoolroom and History

At the opposite end of the upstairs from Mother's bedroom was a second nursery or "schoolroom" with the same generous windows as hers looking out on three sides. This room I shared first with Brewster, my senior by two years, and then with Jack when he was old enough. Occasionally a pillow fight would enliven our truce. But my memories of it are otherwise individual.

I used to lie in one of the two brass bedsteads and see the patterns made on the ceiling after our lights were out, by the old-fashioned gas lights out on the street. Stevenson's "Leery, the Lamplighter" was made real, though we didn't see his counterpart often—a new method may have eliminated daily visits. These windows had one narrow board as a bar across each one. Harry, an older brother, had been known to walk in his sleep; this was a fascinating thing about which to speculate.

Mother would come often and say a good-night prayer. It was sweet of her to come; I never got much of a feeling that it or God was very real for her. Years later when she objected to a patronizing remark that she had never given us much of a faith, she said: "But I always used to come to see you say your prayers." It was an approved ritual which she thought could give us all the necessary background.

The room had a cosy fireplace with Dutch biblical tiles arranged around it. Many was the cheery fire we sat in front of while Mademoiselle read stories in French.

Around the walls just under the ceiling was fastened a series of vivid pictures of principal events in English history. Harold staggering with an arrow in his eye; the galleons of the Armada; King John petulantly signing a parchment; Richard on castle walls somewhere in the Holy Land; Wolfe dying on the plains of Abraham. Whether I got a sense of history or not, I certainly got a sense of violent and strange happenings in a world where anything was possible.

Out the windows to the east where the sun would be coming up as we prepared for school, were the rosy cliffs of East Rock. In my mind Connecticut, though rugged, is a peaceful state. The mountains seem like surprising intrusions and even after all these years I find it difficult to reconcile their grandeur with the rolling acceptance of our wooded hills. However, New Haven has this drama in stone and we looked out on it.

Near those windows and access to a terrace roof was the little bathroom in which, as I've said, were focused the delights of sex.

This "schoolroom" was a happy room in contrast to the training nursery where I'd had so many heavy strokes. A room to which I could usually withdraw for sanctuary when the going got tough below. And over which presided the dainty little square-jawed intellectual whom we knew as Mademoiselle.

Mademoiselle

Mademoiselle was not a beauty. She may never have known the delights of sex, and certainly had borne no children—her training had been literary. She loved her own language and her perfect Parisian pronunciation, which we did our best to imitate. She loved books, reading us Jules Verne and to the older ones Madame de Sevigné. Her voice would tremble with delight as she would mention *L'Isle Mysterieuse.*

Her father, whom she revered, had been a doctor or professional man, but world wars and disturbances had led to her seeking employment in America. In passing, may I pay homage not just to Mademoiselle but to all those whom the marriage market passed by for one reason or another, and who thus dedicated themselves to the souls of those who could afford a governess. I benefitted from a rare tradition.

She was kindly, loving and completely unequipped to cope with the strong wills of us upper-class monsters. Though we were grateful for her care and loved her, it was fun once in a while to tease. She would get excited and talk to herself in a loud voice which, of course, was a great payoff in the game. It was a rare treat that we could thus get and show power over any grown-up.

Proud of her skill, she was a patient, dedicated seamstress and her thumb seemed worn bv the thousands of times she had pushed a needle through cloth by a finger protected by a thimble.

Hard working women of Europe! Your sisters in America are breaking new ground of independence—no longer bound by "a woman's role!"

Her special gift to me, besides the care, was a love of that beautiful language, the ability to read and speak it easily, which, as we shall see, led me as a young man off the ordinary path of my brothers.

Her preference was for Charles, the middle brother, considered a good-looking boy; Jack, too, benefited from her favors. Although not the focus of my jealousy of Jack, I had prickles of discomfort that I couldn't gain the closest affection.

In retrospect, if I was not the favorite, I can realize how fair and open was the number of good strokes I did get when I visited the cosy little room alongside our "schoolroom" where she kept all the little treasures with which a true seamstress equips herself and enriches her work. There she somehow conveyed a deep sense of the wonders of her homeland, her beloved France!

Ah, Mademoiselle!

Downstairs

Downstairs and central to the house was an immense long living room flooded with light, the home of three sumptuous Persian rugs, some elegant stuffed furniture grouped around a fireplace, a grand piano, the Welte Mignon player piano, and so on. Space, luxury, perhaps style.

Ample windows floor to ceiling in the center admitted the light through a conservatory filled with ferns and greenery. French doors opened onto the terrace. Around the walls, as we have seen, galloped divine Greek figures cast from the Parthenon friezes.

For a child a place of magic, wonder and often a place to play.

The blocks could be brought in and spread out. Forts built, around which swarmed the tin soldiers in their multitudes and the artillery attacked or defended.

Or when the player piano was on, we could dance, as I've said. No motions are ever as free and joyful as those uncontaminated by the later thoughts, "How do I look? What will *they* think of me?"

The magic was heightened and epitomized once a year by an amazing celebration known as Christmas.

During the days preceding, we younger ones were not allowed into that room at all where reigned the tree in splendor decorated by the older ones. We had to be blindfolded or go through the back hall for meals. And stockings were hung the night before in the library.

Christmas night—a dark hall down the marble staircase—eerie light as I creep towards it. Shock! . . . the hands point on the grandfather clock—it's not yet midnight—I'm too soon for Santa Claus.

Somehow the stockings get seized at an incredibly early hour. Sticky barley sugar, little puzzles, loot spread through the bed.

And then the procession as finally, to the tune of a hymn, little ones first for once, singing we march in and around the glittering tree where enormous piles of presents loom.

Reading

I would be giving a distorted view of my childhood if I didn't include one of its most important activities, namely reading. Somehow this became such a smooth and solid background for my early life that I don't remember learning to do it and I could say it was a preferred pursuit.

Any hour could find me lost in a fairy story or an adventure book. Soon as childhood advanced, so did my choice and I would wade through Dickens or Scott by the month under Father's approving direction. The *Book of Knowledge,* a many-volumed set of tomes bound in blue, had fascinating illustrations for us all to pore over, but was too disjointed in arrangement for true capture of the mind. The bookworm that I was didn't relish syncopated matter.

In Salem in the summers a rest for reading after lunch was required. So I galloped all the faster through *Bleak House* and *Quentin Durward* to be lavishly stroked for "reading more books than anyone else this summer"!

At ten, with a birthday gift of $10.00, I headed for the second-hand bookstore and, enthralled by the imaginative excitements of Gustave Doré, came home in triumph with a sumptuous copy of *Paradise Lost*. Though I wasn't up to wading through Milton from start to finish, the echoes of his music on every illustrated page rang lovely changes through the years thereafter.

> Wave rolling after wave where way they found.
> If steep, with torrent rapture.

Could it be that a spirit hounded by the You're Not OK—We're OK message given me by the Parent world found total delight in the escape those book covers provided?

Out-of-Doors

Finally, to round out the sketches of our New Haven home, I must mention a foreign country—the out-of-doors. Although I enjoyed it enough while there, and got to know every stick and stone on the wide terrace enclosed by low walls, the curving walks, the grass stretching to the shrubbery behind which were sidewalks and streets, it must be because it was "good for" me that I recoiled often from the command: "Go outside!"

I early learned in many ways to detest whatever was "good for" me, which perhaps began with the "castration" ceremony I've described. Free Child does good things automatically if left free. But if pushed by Parent as I was, and tending in any case to the Vengeful Child position, the very thing I might otherwise have reached for became anathema.

When going to school, as there was no doubt of the necessity of that, with Bruce or Jack, I accepted going far enough into the hinterland, braving the frosty cold till even in mittens the fingers were numb. First I was perched dangerously on the handlebars of Bruce's bike, a procedure that today when automobiles are better known would never be encouraged by safety-minded parents. Then, after being taught by the ever-faithful Smith, careening skillfully enough down steep hills and pushing laboriously on the upgrades, we reached the hallowed precincts of "Hamden Hall."

But once home or on weekends, when books and glowing fireplaces beckoned, when "little wars" were ready to be fought on rug-warmed floors, inside where clothes were never a problem, it was a drag to have to pull on galoshes, sweaters, mittens, wool cap for the mythical value of that fresh air.

Salem

There's a great stretch of land in eastern Connecticut covered with rocks and trees where occasionally old fields still hold off the invasion of the brush, partly protected by many stone walls which meander far and wide. It's well-watered and clear babbling brooks find their way through pebbles and glades to the Connecticut River and the sea. Some branches of our family had held land in Salem for generations—expanded and bought back by the luxurious gentleman, our grandfather Alfred Mitchell.

On the brow of a hill overlooking the smiling Salem valley and miles of view, my own parents had built a rambling one-story structure in the Japanese style as a summer retreat. This my mother called "The Camp."

She had reacted against the luxury of the Tiffany family and the elegance of her mother's homes. Granny had compelled her with the power of the money that paid for it to live in our huge New Haven home. She never wanted that—it was too big and cold in winter.

The walls of the Camp were only one board thick, sheathed with shingles. Like Marie Antoinette, Mother demanded the "simple" life. As our family grew and the older boys needed rooms of their own, the Camp grew. But beyond an unassuming lawn and flower beds began a profusion of grasses, wild flowers, cedars, oaks, rocks in endless variety.

This countryside—wild, intimate, enfolding—has cast its spell over me for many summers, many years, and still holds many of the family who live or visit there.

There I lived in and with a landscape so beautiful that for an eye encouraged to be that of an artist, it was a natural to find and try to capture as many aspects as possible. However, here I think of it more as clothing for the imagination of a child.

You'll remember that the "out-of-doors" seemed somewhat alien and difficult in New Haven. By contrast, Salem was "ours"—the only near neighbors were our own friends; there was endless room. The OK world extended right through nature to the planets we looked at through a telescope and to the stars.

Barefoot

On the very day-long drive to cover the fifty-five miles from New Haven to Salem—over rough incompleted roads, with flat tires, etc.—as we approached the Camp, our excitement grew. The greatest pleasure was to throw off shoes and stockings and feel the cool grass under our feet as we rushed the last yards into a long, luxurious summer.

Barefoot! Tender at first each June, the soles would soon get tough as leather and proudly negotiate pebbly brook bottoms, the blistering asphalt roads that were abuilding, or crackling, prickly spaces between low huckleberry bushes as we fanned out to pick for canning and to stuff snatched surplus hurriedly into the mouth. Farmer Bliven's oats had been cut—bare soles were bleeding on the stubble—better not try that again! Only one spot nonnegotiable!

But oh the puddles on the sandy roads! Liquid mud oozing between each toe. Or dusty hard patches where the fine sand caressed the feet like lovers.

When big games were afoot, blindman's bluff with a dozen players, the wide space between my big toe and the others always gave me away. They called it my "lost toe."

Something about relaxing the discipline of long stockings and encasing shoes, let Free Child out. Time stood still through hot days and cool nights.

The Old Swimmin' Hole

It would be a mistake to say along the length of that marvelous brook that we confined outselves to one best hole, as twenty years later we did. The pool had not yet deepened beyond the stone-arch bridge. Or it was too public near the road to take pants and shirt off. Bathing suits were required, put on in the tall wild grasses and flowers.

A quarter of a mile further down a bend swirled; it was clear. The cows may have waded in off the golden sandspit, down the arching bank to clear away the brush, but somehow politely left no gooey signatures. So there naked we splashed and learned to swim. The kindly sun warmed and dried us.

When I read Kingsley's *Water Babies,* I knew what it felt like. Primevally we descend from the fish!

Childhood; In Summary

Memories—thousands, hundreds of thousands of memories.

I've said my childhood was not all golden because of the pressure of Parent, because of the external threat of punishment becoming internalized in quasi-permanent anxiety.

Yet as I review it, as I bring light and understanding to bear, as I no longer blame dominating or obtuse parents, as I consider their lacks with compassion, it becomes in retrospect more and more glorious and I'm liable to lose perspective in glowing terms.

So let us on without more detail to see how these conditioning script-forming decisions affected the rest of life, notably next that wider circle, the boarding school.

CHAPTER TWO

School—Shyness and Rebellion

A Summary of Script

Perhaps the first school of all wasn't too bad, although I hung back from going at all. I remember a vast fear of that unknown peopled by strange creatures to be known as "friends." I had no idea how to obtain such possessions from lively other boys. Instructions came aplenty, but the label of *shy* given by my family prevented any possibility of carrying them out. Outside people had minds and ideas of their own; how could they be attached?

Early schools had often to be changed because of travel. I found myself in one in Miami one winter. The classrooms were out of doors, cheery with sun and greenery. My early ability to read and remember had put me beyond the same grade as others of like age. More than ever alienated, I said nothing except to the teacher.

Soon the others, boys and girls, with their uncanny perception, had found the term "Living Statue," dancing round me, which I've thought of recently as the words most descriptive of my script, the sweatshirt message. Thus shame was born and on the back, carefully hidden from the world and even from myself, but there nonetheless, were the words: "Go to hell!", i.e., I'm OK—You're Not OK—but I won't say it!

How did I cope with the pain thus produced, a pain which we call shame? Here the choices made earlier in life were guiding as they so often are.

For some people who were given early on the script injunction: Don't Be; Don't Exist, it could have led to the position of despair—I'm Not OK. But by myself or with the tender care of Granny whom I was with quite often that year, I was happy and comfortable.

They are mean to taunt me. But that can only reinforce: There's nothing wrong with me, it's they who are Not OK.

A few sections further on I'll say more on the subject of shame and describe an incident when it was increased in intensity.

Already into the teens, a gawky youth as full of feelings as a volcano, unable to express any of them except positive ones and not many of those except in letters, I went on to Groton.

Groton

The overall impression left of the years at Groton is desperation, though with many good times, good relationships, deep experiences. This contrasts remarkably with the home-written letters of that period, which portray a happy, satisfied boy. I knew what Mother wanted to hear—I was careful to please. Even if pressed, I would have been unable to express what I was feeling. Beyond that an unthinkable alternative would have been transfer to the jungle of a new school. The known bad, which I had learned in some fashion to cope with, was infinitely better than the worse unknown.

Sensing this sharply tempered any criticism I might have expressed, having already discovered that parents sometimes overreact to complaints.

I easily got into my head the academic and general routine of the school, well shepherded by schedules and bells. The classroom periods, with perhaps one exception, were enjoyable learning and lively times with teachers whose characters we, the pupils, early learned to adjust to.

when I was about fifteen. This was later than seems normal with many, perhaps because of the strength of the no-no injunctions with which my childhood had been encased.

I have strong memories of when I was in the "Third Form Year." Images, banished during the active day, probably not even thought of, came as I would lie awake in bed after lights were out and fantasize about sex. This is the only time in life, before or since, that I haven't gone to sleep almost immediately on my head hitting the pillow.

Not knowing either erections or semen yet, the oft-repeated fantasy was that I would urinate into my mother. For fifteen minutes or half an hour, whatever it was, this would form in my head as a delicious, even necessary action.

I remember no negative horror at incest; I had never heard of it. The pleasure was protected in that it was only happening in a pretend world and that I never thought of it during the day.

The emphasis on urine for me who had suffered so much for bedwetting and pants-wetting was significant. It will come into the story later in Paris and with Dr. Brill in New York.

The fact that it was Mother in my fantasy, in spite of all my rebellion and refusal to do her bidding, shows how strong were those erotic ties especially to her—the Red Queen!

However, this was not to last—it faded. Maybe incest is surrounded by too many prohibitions. By the next summer and the next year, there were other preoccupations. And it was not till three years later, at eighteen, that sex flowered again, this time in quite another form.

Art

You've already read of my art instruction at Groton and how deliriously I got into color; how passionately, through Ruskin, I learned to love nature as I saw her.

This led to substantial efforts to duplicate the effects I was observing.

Wandering around the Salem valley in the summers, with its

fields, farmhouses and trees, and especially along the banks of Mitchell Pond, a generous expanse of still, blue water bordered with grass, willow trees and a narrow, pebbly beach, I spent long hours teaching myself every trick of underpainting and overpainting to render those exuberant but delicate hues. The skies were mainly blue, tending to viridian at the horizon, often peopled with clouds of all shapes—the streaks of cirrus, the puffy cumulus and at times the clear blue of the fine cool weather we got in those days.

Sunshine was beloved, too, and how the shadows differed from the lights. The horizon offered endless challenge with its tree-lined edges and soft yet clear perspective.

Years later I was to observe these little landscapes with joy and attempt to explain their purity by saying I was living "purity" then, contrasting it with what I called the "impure" period after masturbation had started in earnest. Knowing how Critical Parent beats on Child, especially when Child is doing what Parent tells it not to do, I now explain the difference by saying that if there is conflict within, the work produced will reflect that and instead of serenity will show war!

Suddenly I made a friend of a classmate, Fuller Potter, a New Yorker, who seemed sophisticated to me. Together we explored with excitement the truly modern movement—Monet, Cezanne, Van Gogh and all the others, burst on us like a fresh breeze. It was no longer necessary or *au fait* for me to prepare panels and rush to seize cloud formations before they dissolved. Color, pigment itself was a frenzy which could be manipulated in moments. My use of square footage of canvas board multiplied many times over.

Shapes appeared and disappeared. If a face or a body could be seen through the chaos, that would give a name to the canvas and thus a suggestion to my family puzzled by the transformation of style. (Their strokes were no longer so sought after as those of a peer.) Darker shades of pure color appeared unmixed with white. My own face glared in solemn doubt in a couple of self-portraits. Whether or not it was masturbation that disturbed me, there was certainly no calm joy evident in the works of those seasons.

During school time of the last year, we had borrowed the use of a classroom from one of the English masters, himself a keen etcher. Alackaday! modernism seemed to lead to lots of spilled paint. Though our friend leaned over backwards in never mentioning it to us, we were told of a few sarcastic but kindly comments on the state of his room. May this passing mention be a trivial payment of gratitude for his forbearing encouragement to creativity!

Competition

I've mentioned the painting done in Salem during long summer vacations. What of the rest of the time; how did I grow?

Tennis was a devouring passion which yet was bent to conform to the script injunctions: *you are awkward; you are slow; you are no athlete!* I spent many hours practicing, driving the ball at a backboard—and got into games whenever brothers or friends or a hired counselor were willing. Our mother had taught us as "little ones" and was quite proud of her agility as the years advanced. I didn't *always* lose, as I dreamed of Tilden, Lacoste or Cochet!

Father approved of competition as favoring growth in skill and "character"! Not content with organizing tournaments when he was there, he kept records of performance at track and, after weeks of preparatory and forced exercises, we were required to compete on one festive day in all the various branches, such as high jump, broad jump, a half-mile run (over to the Woodbridge House and back) and ever so many more.

I lost regularly, not just against bodies of competitors but against past records of those of my own age! One year when practice at that damned clarinet had perhaps strengthened my fingers, I hung my skinny body on a rope longer than anybody else and achieved a totally unexpected triumph!—Kindly-brother Bruce gave me strokes for that for many days thereafter.—But in general the picture was negative.

How skillful is Vengeful Child! I had withdrawn into the bushes below the Camp on one of those track meet days. Heaven knows what reason my conscious mind entertained for thus skulking off, perhaps the pursuit of some bird heard singing below. But a loud thumping in the brush did make my heart jump as a rabbit bounded away.

I returned to the gathering to say I'd heard a rattlesnake down the hill. It wasn't a total fabrication—there had been a noise—I hadn't seen what it was. The rattlesnake was a more useful disruptor than another animal might be.

An aged carpenter working on a new addition to the buildings said he, too, had heard a dry rustle in the leaves. Father said if it had been only Mitch, he wouldn't have paid too much attention, but the old gentleman's confirmation made it important to investigate. The entire company discontinued the athletic event and fanned out over the hillside looking for dangerous reptiles! For a time I was not put down.

Intellectualism

The picture of Salem in the summers during those formative adolescent years wouldn't be complete without a glimpse of our evenings in the living room gathered comfortably around the blazing log fires in the stone fireplace. This was a time when the Bingham brothers absorbed a common trait: intellectualism.

Arguments were long and often heated. No one was preeminent; the game could be called: Let's you and him fight. All polite; all intense.

Mother loved this hour with her brood, savoring the sallies even if cruel, communicating the same pleasure as in childhood: This family is superior because it thinks. Our minds are just a bit better than others. This stroked us.

Years later on the farm, when invited to take part in these gatherings, I was often uneasy. There was a lure, but I had a wife. We called it "spinning" and made some fun of it; the Bingham wives perhaps sensed ulterior satisfactions.

But implanted in my head was a confirmation of an earlier attitude: Observe and think; it will get you through. Cerebrate!

Adult is meant to serve Child and give him better chances. But he can be perverted into thinking his own activity is an end in itself.

Change of Arena

During my early years at Groton I had done pretty well in the classroom; though not first in grades in my form, I had been among the first three or four. I enjoyed the privileges of being on the "over 80" honor roll, among which the chief was being allowed to study in the library rather than in the study hall among the rows and rows of uniform red desks. The library, a place of delight as had been ours at home, permitted wandering anonymously through all the realms of culture—a cave for withdrawal and forgetting Not-OKness.

However, as Jack entered the same school in the lower forms and began to get top marks himself, the old defense against symbiotic competition took over. It would have been unthinkable fratricide to compete with him, jealous as I still was. From somewhere in the recesses of my mind, probably the Little Professor, a new decision emerged. It was kowtowing to authorities if I only accepted their categories of study and boring to spend too much time in preparation. Except for written papers, I finally honed down the preparing time to the twenty minutes before school in the morning, and devoted my evening hours to exploring the tempting world of the French novel or meaningless reenactments in pencil of the war games of childhood.

This mechanism of avoidance of direct competition with another person has lain in wait for me whenever other men seem to choose the same track of prominence as mine. However, it worked as far as Jack is concerned. Once having decided that the esoteric pursuit of French culture made "mine better than yours," I could relax any unpleasant feelings towards him and indeed jealousy, though fastening on others later was never much of a factor with him from then on.

I became proud of my ability in French and skill in skimming for required lessons. Latin was a *bête noir*, due, I believe, to my Vengeful Child having been hooked by a Not-OK teacher of it. In that I could barely "pass," but the other subjects kept me most of the time on that coveted honor roll, though my ranking had fallen to ordinary. I even congratulated myself on my ability to get by.

Self-stroking has always been important in my survival, and the arena having been changed, strokes had to be given for the new activities.

Illness and Miami

I haven't been seriously ill very often in my life and I won't dwell much on these episodes although listed all at once there seem to be quite a number. Each time I can associate the onslaught with periods of great or difficult change.

In early childhood, somewhere along the path of that bed-soiling struggle, a considerable tummy illness struck which led to a delightful sojourn in bed and much coddling. The higher powers talked mysteriously of bad food. The high point in memory was a loving gift from Father of a tall giraffe on squeaky wheels which I cherished from then on.

Just starting life on the farm after a year of marriage, an attack of jaundice ushered in a decade of strenuous physical work.

In the early Moral Re-Armament years a strong jealousy seemed to lead to "rot within" and an almost-fatal attack of appendicitis.

Right in the middle of a liberating three-week T.A. workshop with Hedges Capers, I had to yield to an operation for hemorrhoids! More of that later.

In the traumatic years at Groton, as I've told, the infirmary had me often for colds. In the next-to-last fifth-form year, this became graver. During spring vacation, I was diagnosed as having a spot on the lung and spent those weeks getting good strokes in bed—happily back in the New Haven home under the nurturing ministrations of Joseph, as well as some professional care. For convalescence I was shipped off to Miami with Granny, and thus ushered in one of the happiest spells of my life thus far.

Though a few months only, it seems in retrospect to have packed in enough excitement for several years. I was the center of attention and care of a household. Often in the afternoons Granny gave the use of her limousine and her chauffeur, the rough-and-ready Lynch, to take me to the horse races. I would come back bursting with money and she would say: "But you're supposed to lose, not to win."

In the evenings we played a more modest game of poker patience. And I started reading her aloud the plays of Shakespeare. In the one term we got through most if not all of them.

What I loved was not only the pleasant occupations but the flow of care which was never in doubt. If I accepted too much laconically, she would say: "Purr when you're pleased!"—but that lesson was not truly learned for many decades yet. Symbiotically I assumed she knew I was happy and didn't have to say so.

I knew the final exams for the year at Groton were coming up. Granny would urge some attention to studies. But my method of doing written papers and skimming for the rest seemed adequate. *"I'll show you I can."* Sure enough, I went back for the last couple of weeks of term facing the scepticism of one or two of the less favorably inclined masters and passed through the exams with satisfactory grades.

It was no small joy to tuck into my head that I'd had a royal time, dispensed with the professional teaching and come out just as well at the end.

I was preparing for the final year of revolt.

Open Rebellion

Having gone without much recognition, good or bad, through the earlier years, except for the one incident I've described, the last or graduating year came. Other boys in the sixth form were given responsibilities; I was not, which I resented, though heaven knows I'd given no indication of wanting any and would have denied it if asked.

But the number of trading stamps or abused feelings in my collection was now greater than ever. I could justify cashing them in by going from the passive, silent rebellion of the past to open rebellion.

Spring term; last chance. I took to leaving my sleeping-room study after lights were out, crossing the quarter-mile campus in the dark and joining a group of overt rebels who gathered in the study of one of the masters to listen to music, smoke cigarettes and enunciate profound opinions on the sad condition of the world, the glorious condition of the arts, and the tyranny of Groton.

It was an exciting adventure to drop out the lower floor window or let myself out the big door, circle the campus out of reach of street lights, keep a weather eye out for the watchman and arrive among a group of sympathetic souls bound by our common doctrine of They are Not OK, stay some delightful hours and then run the gauntlet of darkness again in which I felt quite at home, and back to my legal bed. This went on for a whole term without discovery.

Music was a strong part of it. Here I widened my love of Chopin, learned the ecstasy of the Brahms symphonies, and ventured into the world of Rimsky-Korsakoff, Stravinsky and Respeghi's "Fountains and Pines of Rome." Debussy enchanted us with his "*Après-midi d'un Faune*". A whole classical range.

Under this influence with puberty asserting its demands more forcefully and nearer the surface of consciousness, I became slowly aware of a strong romantic attachment to my young artist friend Fuller, who of all had brought me in touch with a hitherto unknown sophistication. He represented the big city of New York, modern—hence rebellious—culture, was friendly, thus giving strokes to one starved for them, and helped to provide an atmosphere where criticism of others could be open and recognized.

The master in whose study this circle was meeting, had open homosexual attachments himself. We talked of Michelangelo and Leonardo. And I, for whom homosexuality was a previously unknown concept, discovered it could be defended and even favored as part of an I'm-OK—They-are-Not-OK hostility towards the reigning powers of the school.

For me it never went to any physical acts and by the next year in Paris, the heterosexual interest was again titillating and commanded most of my attention. When on the second year's boat to Europe a young musician proposed sharing a room, I felt vaguely repelled and lost his incipient friendship by refusing the offer.

I can speak for no one but myself but believe a large part of the attraction to homosexuality that thrilling year was that it was part of what Parent was against and my by now open I'm OK—They are Not OK welcomed all the apparatus of revolt.

The well-known headmaster, Dr. Endicott Peabody, on whose bald head I used to vent my vengeful feelings from afar when I gazed thereon in chapel, sensed something was going on that year that conflicted with the godliness he constantly strove for. One beautiful spring Sunday his sermon was a blast against the notorious Oscar Wilde who even "wore carnations in his buttonhole." After the service we promptly made our way to the village florist and proudly sported white carnations thereafter in ours!

I mentioned smoking. The penalty for being caught was expulsion. I believe I started on one of the train trips to or from school. This, too, became a delight which we indulged at those nocturnal gatherings. I soon carried cigarettes defiantly in my pocket and cockily found my fingers nicotine-stained. These acts seem so provocative as to be obvious moves in a hard game of Kick Me. However, so colorless had been my previous sojourn in the school, so much had I become a part of the wallpaper that no one noticed anything until the final episodes after our formal graduation ceremonies had been held.

The Novels and Sex

I mentioned reading French novels. While later in Paris was the time for delving profoundly into Proust and the English Aldous Huxley, at Groton I got well into Balzac. His romantic portrayal of young Lucien de Rubempré making his way in the world of the big city, thrilled me in anticipation.

One book especially which delighted me at that time was *Révolte des Anges (Revolt of the Angels)* by Anatole France. My rebel Child thrilled at the fantasy of the overthrow of the heavenly powers and the enthronement of Lucifer. Beyond that the sex episodes made it all seem too good to be true, and I longed for the instant when I would be thus ensconced with a lovely lady. His tone of light irony and surprise fitted in well with one who lacked confidence that his ability could carry off any such situation. In the world he portrayed, it all seemed to happen so naturally, it was unnecessary to wonder about how.

This seemed to fit in easily with and be a part of the sexuality which was now budding so strongly. I never thought of having to side for heterosexuality or for homosexuality as far as being one or the other. My mutinous Child told me they were all excellent because disapproved of by the authorities.

Final Fling

If my rebellious acts of that last term had been unconsciously designed to reap a kick, they had failed of their objective. Escalation would be needed but a prudent voice inside my head suggested waiting until after the graduation. Thus any risk I take is usually calculated and doesn't push to the point of self-harm.

Our little circle boarded a train for Boston, went to the afternoon symphony to absorb the gyrations of Koussevitsky, and had supper at the Ritz Carlton. There I consumed escargots in front of a group of attentive waiters (I've been partial to escargots ever since), consumed a moderate amount of alcohol (the Prohibition amendment hadn't yet been repealed), and went innocently to bed in a respectable hotel. The next day we boarded the morning train and returned peacefully to school, which had not yet dismissed its pupils for the summer.

Meanwhile, when a good-night check had revealed our

absence—I had always previously held back my nocturnal excursions until after that verifying count—the alarm was sounded. The master, too, was found to be missing. Our parents were notified and the steamships departing for Paris were contacted to see if I were aboard—I had already evidently talked up my longing for that Elysian isle.

When I heard about this, I was amazed that anyone would think I would thus rashly cut my lines of supply. My New England upbringing (Adaptive Child) has always carefully seen to it that bread and butter would be provided. And I would certainly not rush off to Europe without parental assurance that my allowance would be faithfully maintained!

We were met with indignation. Mr. X, an enemy who was supposed to be head of secret intelligence and to know all that went on, backed me up against a wall and purple-faced gave a blast of You are Not OK. Later that evening we sat in suspense through a good-bye talk to the sixth form in the headmaster's study. The offending master had already been given his walking papers and left. (He disappeared to an obscure life as an actor in Hollywood.) At the end the class was dismissed, but we were requested to stay.

A loud and shaking roar of disapproval. What could the poor man do? The hour was late for imposing sanctions.

So once more we left with luggage for home, once more we visited Boston, this time to a speakeasy and much hard liquor consumed in a hotel room. Some of us were sick. Alcohol depresses me and I didn't enjoy this rather sordid finale. I like control and have rarely repeated losing it as that night.

Washington

Almost immediately I went alone to Washington to see Father and ask his permission to go to Europe in the fall to study art. He was in the Senate then but used the hot early-summer weekends to play golf with his cronies, conservative Republicans like himself. We were out at the fashionable Burning Tree Club and I was permitted to caddy. Back in the locker room, I heard him say to Senator Hale, over the partition which separated us while they dressed, "I don't know what to do with him."

At that time hippies and the counterculture were far from being heard of, and although the Bohemia of Paris had attracted many Americans, parents could safely puzzle over the treatment of their rebel children without loss of seeming *savoir faire*.

As we drove together back to our lodging, he asked me a crucial burning question: would I be willing to give up going to Paris and settle for the Yale Art School in New Haven. He had evidently accepted the inevitable of my career in painting but wished I could assimilate the rather more solidly respectable methods of that safer institution.

My heart sank; farewell to the dream!

As I've said, I had no idea of cutting the source of funds and venturing to far places without support. It hurt but I answered, "Yes."

He replied: "I was hoping you'd say that. In that case, you can go." Oh joy! The dream would come true.

Strangely, instead of the flow of grateful warmth which might have brought us closer, I felt as I travelled back to Salem for the summer, a curious contempt. He hadn't kicked when he could have. I, who had learned to expect negative knocks whenever I made close contact with those others identified as Parent, didn't know how to respond with healthy love to a Nurturing Parent voice: "Go, my child, and enjoy what you want." *The world in the person of Father had turned out to be more nurturing than my negative expectation!*

Masturbation

Whether it was during that particular summer or earlier, I'm not quite sure, I was exploring the delights of masturbation. I had heard vaguely at school of boys doing things together.

Very privately I experimented in the warmth of a hot bath. Orgasm seemed unbelievable. My pleasures for years had come uniquely from mind and appreciation of the flood of sensations through eyes and ears distilled in thought and a cultural snobbism: my sensitivity is greater than yours. The hand was used for brush and pencil to serve the eye—not for sensation itself. The hungry body slowly discovered forbidden parts.

Not for long was this unassociated with another person, at least a dream figure.

We had a maid in those years, a fair-haired girl from Germany, shy, impulsive, no plastic beauty. I never thought of her as a possible wife and for this I apologize at this late date. I was far too scared to think of her as a mistress. But huddled under the sheets I masturbated at night or had wet dreams knowing she would come the next day to make the bed. I find it hard in these latter years to think I expected some other person to do that for me, but such is the lethargy of upper-class reliance on servitude!

Golden promise, she was married to someone in Germany later and has a son whom she adores.

We talk about self-centeredness and self-love. It seems we usually want a reflector, even if only an imaginary one, to connect with another person the strokes that otherwise couldn't quench that endless thirst.

CHAPTER THREE

Solitary Student

Paris

Lured on by the *Révolte des Anges* of Anatole France, full of hope that at last I would be free of the Not OKness, that I would find, though vague as to detail, a love where sex would be spontaneous and the dreams come true, I sailed with Fuller for Paris, the fairy city, Father, Mother and family gloriously left behind.

I was armed with a generous letter of credit, a promise of allowances to come, and though brokers and bankers were jumping out of skyscraper windows—it was the dread fall of 1929—I was rather indifferent to this aspect of the news. I was concerned mostly with my own pleasure. The photographs of those years show a lonely, rather pinched face under the curly hair.

To show what I may have looked like in those years, herewith a limerick—composed at a party a couple of years later where each in turn adds a line, the subject being the one nonparticipant as the little poem goes round the circle:

Said Mitch looking over his easel,
'Your face is the face of a weasel
But I really don't care
If I paint you all hair
For in Rome I have taken the Prixle'.

This clever rhyme shows how the subconscious of those in the game by switching subjects, "you" (other) instead of "you" (Mitch), etc., can allow the true feelings of the observer to come out.

Looking back on those three part years in Europe—I used to come back in the summers—I think of them with especial pleasure. Lonely as all get out, unable to make relevant contact with another soul, my pursuit of art was so avid as to provide sufficient strokes for survival and lead from one place to another.

I have in my possession a little seascape done the third year in Greece. It is almost nothing but calm blue sea and cloudless sky—with a sail in the mid-distance, a plume of steamship smoke, a few blurs of white gull. Infinity, peace—almost nothing and yet cherishable; my Mother kept it by her; now it hangs near my desk—symbolic of the emptiness yet fullness of those painful years.

There were, however, events that marked the psychic adventure I was embarked on—for the first time in my life on my own.

Fuller Potter soon settled in with a sad-faced English girl named Mae, to explore the delights of sex. I found myself alone in a tiny fifth floor garret overlooking the Tour Eiffel, which yet had enough room to store paintings, masturbate and sleep in. André L'Hôte was our only teacher, a fascinating talker and logical mind who was attempting to academize the inventiveness of the Cubists and the Fauves.

Otherwise we found haven at La Grande Chaumière, where one could paint indefinitely and go to sketch classes and draw from life in the evenings, all without a teacher. Work, work, work!

Weekends at the Louvre and in the evenings thrilling concerts at the Théatre des Champs Elysées, after which we would walk across Paris at night to the Left Bank.

Fuller didn't understand French nor get much from L'Hôte. The second year he stayed in New York and I was more isolated than ever as I moved to the slopes of Montmartre.

Nudes

When I had walked into André L'Hôte's class for the first time and saw a nude woman posing on the stand, it was a shock from which I almost physically recoiled. For literally the first time in the flesh that which I had dreamed of was revealed.

I couldn't meet her eye. That initial canvas I carefully made of the head, neck and upper bust was not a bad likeness, though unappreciated by the Cubist; I sought safety in portraying the person.

These reactions took time to get over. As the Cubist method is to chop up the lovely body into lines and angles, this soon became another way to disguise the interest in what was so invitingly presented. I could ignore what I saw by simplifying it.

Fuller, as I've said, took one way out of the temptations thus exposed. It seemed impossible to me and I wasn't sure I would want anyway to be closeted with a stranger.

Eric Berne has suggested in *Sex and Human Loving* that satisfying intercourse will hardly be possible unless on each side there is a hook to the earliest loved one of childhood—some reminder, some feature that recalls the safety, the comfort of home or the womb. In my case with my script of "You'll *never* make it," I doubt if I could even get close to a woman without that relaxing and permitting signal from what she is to my subconscious. We'll see as the story develops. But that first year went by in spite of anguish in solitude without closer approach, though many nudes were paraded before my eye in the course of the year.

The Little Fur Piece

I had early learned to love cafés, the privilege of sitting as many hours as one wanted either discussing the profundities of art or life with companions, or simply watching the passers-by in the vague hope that here would come the great adventure. They seemed crowded at any hour, especially those the first year in Montparnasse, which had become well-known for the great who had earlier frequented them, Le Dôme, La Rotonde and others. These at that time were full of students from the wild days of Berlin, Europe and the world, nondescript, rootless characters who shared in an indeterminate revolt. More rarely we went to the Closerie des Lilacs nearer the Sorbonne which seemed more uniquely French.

In Montmartre, on the other hand, on the frontier between the downtown of business and the target area of nightlife hunters who late every evening roared up the hill in taxis in search of excitement, I was immersed in a more bourgeois environment. Meals at favorite places where I had my own napkin ring and bottle of wine, and was thought to be "Anglais" as no American was known to be so silent. Afterwards sipping the coffee and a brandy—I favored Martel Triple Star—in glittering glass establishments which seemed to have no character of their own.

In one of these one day I did finally pick up a youngish French girl, one of two sitting together, and invited her up to my room, this room a wall-papered, modernistic studio with large windows looking up to the Sacré Coeur, where I had been striving to create paintings of the quality of Vermeer and De Hooch—André L'Hôte having been left behind as too scholastic—he insisted on cubist work.

I managed to convey to the lady I was after sex and, although she never took off her clothes, something did happen. Exactly what is a subject of dispute.

My memory is that I urinated into her, a realization of the fantasies of school days. Dr. Brill, to whom I went for psychoanalysis and about whom you'll read when I'm covering the return years back in the United States, insisted this was a physical impossibility and couldn't have happened associated with an erection. Mainly from this incident, I believe, he deduced my divorce from reality and pronounced the diagnosis of schizophrenia, as we shall see.

My memory is that this was painful to the young woman and that, by mutual consent, although I continued to see her for some time, we didn't venture to renew the hurtful attempt. I gave her some francs and enjoyed helping her pick out a little red fox fur piece, with which she draped the rather slight body, which I never learned to know.

She only permitted me to see her at stated times, mostly at meals or in cafés and I got to know her friend also. The impression I'm left with is of a sad, small personality from the provinces, caught as so many are between the jaws of cruel economic forces, insisting on survival, probably accountable to a master pimp who gave her direction. Doubtless to her I was a fairly faceless enigma. A brunette with a little hooked nose, her profile loomed whitely out of a turbulent storm-tossed landscape done at that time, which profile recalls the mother I had safely left across the Atlantic! Evidently there was enough resemblance to have permitted the contact at all.

About the reality of that episode. I was so ashamed of it that I only revealed it to Dr. Brill and never to my wife, until late in our marriage, when Moral Re-Armament brought in the concept of *absolute* honesty. She surprised me by saying: "I told you everything; why didn't you tell me?" But I told it as a reality that had happened.

Now that through TA my Adult is strengthened and I can look more objectively at these occurrences of shame and emotion, I can say: I don't honestly know what did happen. What I see is a loser pattern, a Victim pattern which makes the most of certain defeats, which, though I had determined: "I'll show you I can," is nevertheless led to accept "You Never Will."

Improvement through the psychoanalytic treatment did lead to marriage, as we shall see, and got me further along the dreamed-of path. However, let me not anticipate the story too extensively!

Mother's Visit

One early spring day I received a letter from Mother announcing that she was coming over and would pay me a visit, we might go to England together, and so on.

It seemed an ordinary enough thing. Though rebelling

against it, I had put myself regularly under her eye and, thus, control each summer. But the little lady of Montmartre was still fresh in my mind. This was Paris where the no-no things were encouraged, the territory where Child could act as he pleased. Perhaps it was threatening to have Parent intrude a personal representative upon Child's playground.

As the day of her boat train drew near, I grew agitated and preoccupied. Crossing one of those busy streets near La Madeleine with my head down, I stepped right in front of a taxi! He stopped sharply and I was knocked down with a bad bruise on the shin, but no worse, as reality broke brutally in on my dream. I apologized to a voluble driver. He went on while I recovered poise and body sufficiently to act reasonably when she came.

As I've said, I'm not ordinarily suicidal. Perhaps on this occasion punishment had to be inflicted before I could meet the Red Queen face to face.

Rue de Lappe

Of the dozen or so other people who crossed my path in the years in France, as people, not just as background, I'll give an example to show my inability to make and maintain a friendship based on the exchange of positive strokes, which after all is the only worthwhile kind. Later I was to feel as though a demon pushed me to give negatives and not foster positives. And only most recently do I understand the nature of the witch's curse or script based on a decision of my own childhood that thus I must be and thus I must act.

I used to go to Tiffany & Co. in Paris to cash checks with which to replenish the limited funds needed for my simple requirements. A kindly middle-aged Frenchman employed there who handled these took an interest in me. One day he invited me to his home for dinner and to meet his attractive wife. I went to a pleasant meal.

On the balcony afterwards, overlooking the glittering lights of the city, he pointed with a smile to one line of lamps as marking the location of the Rue de Lappe, notorious for the prostitutes who frequented it. Prompted by my devil and without Adult thought, I replied quick as a wink: "Pas si loin de chez vous!" ("Not so far from your home!"). Hardly a remark calculated to further the very friendship I appreciated and needed. Sure enough, he didn't invite me again.

Provence, the Alps, Greece, Italy, England

Although tempted to dwell on all the pleasant places I visited in those years, drunk with the beauty of the Alps, of the hills and plains of Provence where I seemed to live inside a perpetual Cezanne or Van Gogh, of the Parthenon with its special glow in the sun, or of the little port of Patras on the Gulf of Corinth, where freighters come in from every part of the world, I don't think ecstatic descriptions are the same as the incidents related to script which show a spirit bound but struggling to be free.

In Patras where I made friends with a versatile young Greek, anxious to improve his skill in English, he did his best in the atmosphere of a big, grubby restaurant where he devoured fish heads with relish, to get me to accept an assignation with a dark-haired maiden of the town. He labored in vain as the script prohibition was fortified by the failure of the past and I was not overly anxious to tempt the unknowns of the situation.

I might mention, however, the visit to England where my mother's only sister, my "Aunt Charley," graciously invited me to spend a few days in her luxurious home in Dorking with her husband, the well-known astronomer-writer Sir James Jeans, and her daughter Olivia, our only first cousin.

It had been long since the starched collars of Groton and I arrived with a "stiff" shirt and studs but no collar, expected to "dress" for dinner! A pitying uncle lent me his with a smile, but his neck was several sizes larger and the collar hung down that awkward evening. Aunt Charley told me the dress shirt would not be needed for the rest of the visit; Olivia only looked.

The next morning I was resting comfortably in the bed of an

elegant room with time still before breakfast when the door opened and I was unconscionably startled to have a neatly-uniformed, pink-cheeked young maid walk in with a cup of tea! I wasn't used to such invasions of my privacy.

I had hoped to build some friendship with Olivia, exactly my own age. She spent most of the time, however, in her room from whence poured the strains of all the latest jazz records, of which I knew nothing. At meals I mentioned the subjects of my own interests. Just then the melodies of the poet Swinburne were reaching an ear already trained by Keats and Tennyson and I enthused over his running meters. She repeated the name "Swinburne!" with such scorn that I understood myself to be hopelessly sentimental and totally Not-OK.

In more extensive conversations with Aunt Charley—the others in the family had by that time abandoned me to her as being responsible for my being there, although I thrilled at Sir James' pouring out of his soul in Bach fugues on the organ—I told her of my endeavors in painting. She had had some success in having poetry published. Thinking it facetious, I made the error of calling myself "a bad artist." She jumped on that with full Parent: "How could anyone with so little training who was just beginning dare to call themselves either bad or good?" I should certainly attend the proper schools in England attached to the Royal Academy!

Alas, this turned out to be a rather tragic household. Olivia wound up with a broken marriage and arthritis. Charley died a few years later of cancer of the breast. Sir James did better in overcoming his shyness and found another talented organist to marry and with whom to brighten his later years.

I went back to my solitary life and gleefully gathered a few negative strokes from my aunt's letters, which shows the continuing strength of my reliance on these knockdowns. Indeed I was to gather them for many years yet.

CHAPTER FOUR

Psychoanalysand in New York

I suppose I must have been profoundly discouraged by the failures and loneliness of Europe. But it's characteristic of the basic Vengeful Child position not to admit such weaknesses. Though I did know there was something wrong with me, I would call it shyness if I had to put a name to it. I was working hard still at that satisfying art and never had a thought that I wouldn't be famous some day; "I may not be OK but my art is!"

Brother Alf, unmarried still, was going to be busy starting a radical magazine, *Common Sense,* in those New Deal years and invited me to share the expense of an apartment with him. We wound up on Stuyvesant Square, the 15th Street side; I can almost locate the old house now. It belonged or was leased to two Jewish doctors, man and wife, who had subleased it to us furnished.

From the point of view of my *psychic adventure,* however, the most striking feature of this apartment, with the long windows and dusty window frames, was a bookshelf full of the entire collected works of Sigmund Freud, which the good doctors had bought and had to store somewhere. I devoured them all!

Freud was not an unknown name to me. I had been shocked in Paris by a discussion with an older student. We told our dreams and mine timidly put forth was of skyscrapers rising heavenward in perspective round my head—amusedly diagnosed by him as a sexual one. Though masturbating regularly, my sexual life was ferociously private and I didn't enjoy the public exposure.

More such discussions ensued. I learned about sadism and masochism. The young man, according to his own account (we didn't witness it), enjoyed beating his mistress with a whip. Though in my wildest fantasies I couldn't have done such a thing and wouldn't have wanted to, I accepted that there were people strange enough to do so.

So by the time I found Freud in the bookcase and bought his *Introductory Lectures*, I felt what I had felt earlier with Anatole France, Proust and Balzac, a new world opening up with all the usual thrilling implications of OKness right around the corner.

Samson

My brother with some money and surrounded by every type who wanted to ride the crest of revolution, brought home a man who somehow found me a sympathetic listener. I would take him to an occasional meal, where he would pour out his doctrine. Leon Samson was a special-splinter Communist who was so unique there was only one in his "Party."

Authoritative about every phase of the Party's activities, flinging many names that were new to me, like Sydney Hook and Emma Goldman, he had reduced the dialectic to theatre and explained that in America all was farce. A strong player of the Ain't It Awful game, the awfulness was that nothing could be tragic or comic as history was meant to be, it all became farce.

I listened—"Living Statue" is good at that. He felt encouraged that he had a disciple.

It developed that he had managed to obtain the services (for nothing) of the eminent psychoanalyst, A.A. Brill, translator of Freud into English, who was safely ensconced in one of the apartment towers of Central Park West and kept mysterious track of souls during office hours.

If Samson could see Brill and talk familiarly about him, so could I! This established a line of possible action because the way was shown in which I might approach a living representative and authority of the august but hitherto unapproachable world of ideas at their source.

Here, as both before and since, was a challenging new opportunity to learn, to experience, where Father, my model, the famous explorer, gave the go-ahead with his example. My usual shyness put aside, without even much trepidation as I recall, I not only obtained an interview but agreed speedily to visit Dr. Brill for an hour once a week for which I was to pay the, for me, quite generous sum of $300 a month. Curiosity and the ever-beckoning hope of psychic improvement (I had ample permission in my script for that) were stronger than my usual parsimony.

Samson, according to Dr. Brill, was a very disturbed individual. Not many months later he wound up in an institution. The staff observed him through a one-way window, talking to himself, etc. Brill told me about it as though those were final observations. Sure enough, Samson expired there not long after.

Brill

When I first went into the quiet office—no one else about, and found myself talking to this dignified elderly gentleman, who with his little beard below the lower lip and massive face looked like nothing less than one of Rembrandt's most distinguished burghers, I was surprised not to be put on a couch. But no, I sat on the other side of a desk and we looked at each other.

I was full of the terms I had reaped so richly in the collected works. "No, no, you have it all wrong!" I had tried self-diagnosis at once. A patient is supposed to get gradually indoctrinated and through attachment to the therapist, the "transference," brought gradually to change. Here I was trying to jump through all the hoops at once!

I was soon told that I was "schizophrenic." The best that could be hoped for was that I learn to "maintain" myself in society. Many people did and there was no reason I couldn't under his supervision.

You may think this distressed me greatly and that this label, which I do believe was hardly deserved, did me great harm. Actually I hadn't enough background to let it. It was never suggested I be institutionalized. The term didn't seem all that heavy. By the time a couple of years later that I married and he told me I was cured, I thought little of it and never let it interfere with any plan I had.

Brill also told me I had to do more than paint at home in the apartment and come to him. Samson was too disturbed to be a worthwhile companion. I should meet many people—that was what I wanted—by taking part in activities where people would be.

He suggested two areas. One: going back to art school. I demurred at submitting to teachers whose work I didn't fancy, when I had been working well on my own! But with his point I couldn't argue. I was going there to meet folk, not primarily to learn. He recommended the Art Student's League.

The other was dancing lessons at the celebrated school of Arthur Murray. He told of patients who were enjoying that. For this I was nothing loath, as I knew I knew nothing of dancing, having plodded painfully around the floor at many a debutante party in Washington in the years when Father was in the Senate and I was a teenager on vacation.

In thinking back to my "analysis," I am aware that the purpose is to explore the unconscious of the patient. And in truth I babbled on endlessly—putting him sometimes to sleep, which I thought of as part of the treatment—and brought forth many a dream as required.

In those years a recurring one was being back in school subject to the tyranny I hated.

But unorthodoxically I was thus also told what to do. Knowing my weakness and my pain and having put my life into hands I judged to be more capable than mine, it didn't occur to me that I had any option but to accept the suggestions.

Art Student Again

Soon I became familiar with the routine at that ornate, heavy, dirty building on 57th Street, where art could supposedly be learned. The stairs, the studios—I was used to nude models by then—and more usefully for my purpose, the noisy cafeteria, where we could take our breaks, meet each other, and prolong those breaks over cups of coffee and talk and talk and talk about art. Boys and girls. I became accepted as perhaps never before in any group.

Dancing School

At Arthur Murray's, where I would go in the late afternoon, I found a simple world of learning rhythm and steps in the company of a patient, attentive girl. Alone together in a bare room, where any kind of music we required was piped in, from tango to tap, we worked at and found an answer to the injunction: Be Awkward. I became quite skilled and mastered one step after another.

I was told the rule was that the girls weren't supposed to date the clients after hours. And with my Adaptive Child so much in control—A Please Me driver predominant—it didn't occur to me that that was one rule probably made to be broken. The fear wouldn't break that barrier, though the girl was pleasant and seemed to become somewhat attached to me. It was always the same one.

Looking back and knowing how promiscuous I already was in mind, I can only say that until permission is somehow given, no amount of desire can break the script injunction: You will *never* attain.

Brill, Continued

These were not ideas that Dr. Brill or any orthodox psychoanalyst would be familiar with. It took the genius of Eric

Berne later to underline the massive intervention of script on people who thought they controlled their own lives.

Brill himself hurtled against the very prohibitions that bound me. I had come to him saying I wanted to sleep with the girls.

You want to—so why don't you? Why don't you? Why don't you?

As a psychoanalyst he was committed to bringing light onto the root causes of behavior stemming from the Oedipus relationship. There wasn't lack of evidence in my case—classic attachment to mother, jealousy of brother, an inhibited oral stage, anal stage, etc., etc.

Why don't you?

But he wasn't only an analyst and a man in Critical Parent ego state, he believed the resistance could be beaten down by the assertion of power. You do it.

My resistance mounted and whatever he might say, Vengeful Child quickly said to itself: "Like hell I will!" Overwhelming fear was the symptom not to be denied at any moment when I was actually in the presence of an attractive female.

Neither the lovely dancing partner any more than the eager maidens who listened to my art lore on 57th Street were *in my script!* Permission was not yet given inside my head!

CHAPTER FIVE

Marriage

Lady Met

Through this frustrating impasse and struggle the pressure mounted. Something was bound to give. I couldn't have foreseen what or how.

On one of the visits to Salem, visits which though prolonged from summer to summer never seemed to get anywhere, the telephone rang. Cousin Anna Nevins, a spinster who lived in a fabulous mansion near the shore in Waterford, had a great niece, Norris, who wanted to go to the yearly *boatrace* dance. Could one of the Bingham brothers take her? I was the only one at home or free. So fate descended.

Of the dance itself I remember not a thing, but of part of the conversation much. It went on including a long spell in the pantry at the Nevins' home, until three in the morning. We had much to confide and willing ears into which to pour the confidences.

I know I complained: Ain't It Awful is an easy and attractive game to play. But what I chose to murmur at on that particular occasion is also lost.

Norris had a difficult home life; she was working as a secretary on Wall Street. Her father, himself a bond expert in the prestigious firm of Brown Brothers-Harriman, commuted daily to their little home in Port Washington on the northern shore. He was hell-fire and damnation when it came to the supervision of an only daughter, one of the few descendants in an old New York-New England family. We discovered ourselves to be fourth cousins, knowing the same boarding school backgrounds and WASP patterns of life. She had five other family names of which the one most used was Norris.

She had recently been engaged to an attractive Harvard man but that had rather inexplicably and tragically broken. I gathered that in the southern tradition—her mother was of a famous Virginia line—she was what is known as a belle with many beaus.

Frank, her father, consumed a quart of whiskey upon returning from work each evening. He was not averse to beating his daughter with a strap.

For once I wasn't afraid. Here was a damsel in distress who needed protection, deliverance from a dragon at home. Without words but deep within the mechanism which would project me into that set of relationships known as the "Karpman Rescue Triangle" was already at work. This basic structure is comprised of the three positions of Rescuer, Persecutor and Victim. Perhaps all human disputes can be analysed with these three elements, as Steiner sums them up: Rescuer: I'm OK—You're Not OK but I'll try to help you; Persecutor: I'm OK—You're Not OK and it's your fault; Victim: I'm Not OK—You're OK, help me!

We began to see each other.

In effect, what I was preparing to do was to exchange one prison for another. I had been bound by: You are shy; You will *never* attain. The other, the prison of relationships which the Karpman Triangle so well describes, is found by millions to give their only options where dealings with other humans are concerned.

It was as though the Critical Parent installed in my head was saying: "Okay, you can get close to a woman, but it won't be the real attainment you dream of because you will still wind up in your preferred position of Victim and none of the three positions are really free or intimate.

I wouldn't know consciously for many years what the subconscious seemed to know instinctively, that one of the most significant features of the Karpman Triangle is the *Switch*, i.e., that we switch readily from one point on the triangle to another—from Rescuer we naturally become Persecutor or Victim, and so on. They are interchangeable positions.

I may mention here a variant description of behavior which also centers around the friction between people. Instead of a triangle, Jacqui Schiff, a motherly wonder who specializes in curing the most difficult, prefers to use a hexagon of different positions as follows: "Caretaker, Angry Righteous, Woeful Righteous, Hard Worker, Woeful Wrongdoer, Angry Wrongdoer." The point is we still switch from one position to another. And I was still subconsciously searching for a not-OK position.

OKness isn't found by accident or even a vague prayer: "Oh God, give me a good life." It's found by understanding and thought. "Let there be light!"

Courtship and Sex

I soon found myself going out on the commuter's joggly train to visit Norris's home. Her parents were polite and I was positive in return. They were generous hosts and gave me many a tasty meal in the cosy suburban house. From my perch of new-found Freudian doctrine I felt superior and that I could handle any situation that might arise. When any parental protests were made about being out too late or too often, I calmly ignored them and pressed Norris for added time.

Rebecca, her mother, was gracious and accepting. We soon developed a friendship which lasted through the ups and downs of thirty years. Frank was dry, cool, but not hostile. He had disliked the Harvard man; perhaps he preferred a suitor for his daughter who would stand up to him. I never got more than a few positive strokes from him in the years I knew him, but he was careful to avoid any negatives. The fuel for the fire came from the accounts of his daughter; the feud had a reality for them which didn't require a third party.

Beyond the talks that Norris and I were having, I was happy to find that the dancing lessons were paying off. She was light on her feet and learned quickly to follow all the intricacies with which Arthur Murray's had fortified me. At that time the Childs chain had a generously large restaurant on 59th Street with an orchestra. We spent evening after evening adjusting in rhythm to each other. The floor was never too crowded; it was an unaccustomed but intoxicating sensation to feel that I had the lead part in a performance which could be admired. And, indeed, when we danced elsewhere in front of family or friends, there came strokes of encouragement and praise.

We began to sit together in Central Park. My hands got bolder.

Soon my mind pushed to go further. Dr. Brill was urging it, too, and he arranged a visit for Norris to a leading woman gynecologist so that nature could be circumvented and we could go all the way without untoward complications.

Now I must draw a veil over many intimate experiences, as Norris is still very much alive and I need to respect her privacy. It must suffice to say that for the first time, and for quite a number of years, things went well with a normal number of disappointments. Later we'll come to times when they no longer did go well.

However, all the way through these first "happy" years the deep-seated injunction "Don't Feel" crippled my appreciation and actually prevented me from experiencing all that was successfully happening! You may not believe it but evidently it is possible to do things without perceiving all that goes with them!

Vengeful Child, as I said in telling of my childhood dreams, doesn't have the power to go against the very strongest authorities in the head, so he works out a compromise. I was acting out: I'll Show You I Can; but I was also obeying: Don't Feel.

Herself—A Ceremony

One day Norris asked, "When are we going to get married?" I was already deeply attached; it was a question of time. There were the families to consider—it would be unthinkable not to include them all. A spring wedding at Waterford was arranged under the aegis of the delightful Nevins great-aunts. Many invitations were sent out.

Vengeful Child couldn't stem this flood of the accepted thing which had been set in motion. But along with Norris I did discard any usual marriage service and privately drew up a heady combination of Nietzsche and Kahlil Gibran with which to assert some independence.

What was she like, this girl with whom I was thus preparing to link my life?

Norris had been told at some early point in her life that she looked like Mary Astor, the movie star! With a tilting Nevins nose, a jutting chin, bobbed hair and a lively expression, she was persuaded of her attractions which, of course, is more than half the battle. It's the doubt of her looks that makes the wallflower rather than the actual features, just as a woman often stroked for her beauty will be beautiful. If you doubt this, try to describe actually what makes for the beauty in the outstanding women you know. However, in making such a bold statement perhaps I should admit that now for me all women are beautiful, except for the viragos, and all can be without exception.

One portrait of her on which I lavished much time, shows a fair young girl, not too sure of herself, gazing out at the artist with puzzled round eyes, as much as to say: "What's this I've gotten myself into?"

Another one, by a window wearing a hat with stylish slant, glares out at the world somewhat vengefully. In still another, standing upright in a red dress, she's in full command of her charms. Thus all unconsciously I caught the varied ego states in which, like all humans, her spirit could dwell.

She talked well and used all the thoughts she had—unlike myself in company who banishes them the minute their privacy is threatened. So I easily allowed her the social ascendancy and left the initiatives in making and keeping friends with her.

This great day dawned—May 29th, 1935.

Afterwards I learned of the shock my poor mother-in-law had when instead of the familiar words that soothe us with their promises, unaccustomed phrases denoting especial responsibility and not taking too much for granted came from the lips of brother Bruce, the officiating minister. He had been ordained only a short time before, thus was performing virtually his first official function. I feel badly even now that I took advantage of his good nature, as so often in earlier years, and imposed a service he would never have chosen himself.

Fuller Potter had come, graciously, to be best man.

My own memory of the service is brief. Probably I'll Show You was cashing in a number of stamps.

There was a reception afterwards in the generous garden, with many familiar faces and amiable smiles for the occasion.

One of Norris's former beaus had appeared. She spent what I thought was considerable time excitedly running after him. My Child was yelping: "Hey, what about me? Is not this my day, our day?"

However, on this of all days and events, I wasn't about to break the spell of silence and neither then nor afterwards say what I'd felt. A dull thud of jealousy weighed me down and shows in the photos taken that afternoon. Basically behind this was a fear: you can't say anything; that'll show you up as Not OK. It has taken me decades to learn that openness about such weaknesses will open the other person's heart like nothing else.

Eventually we changed into "going-away" clothes and through some scattered showers of rice backed hastily out the gate in our new car. Down an embankment—another car was speeding on the highway. But I braked in time and away we sped, having given the guests a considerable surge of unexpected adrenalin, as they thought for a second they were witnessing a tragic start for the marriage.

Afterwards

I can't call the next weeks a honeymoon, as honeymoon it

wasn't. Blissful lovers united, the problems of the world temporarily set aside as they enjoy each other in some lavish setting, is the picture the word conveys.

We had arranged to have the Camp to ourselves. Why did I choose that rather than going away somewhere? I am uncomfortably reminded that it had been the sense of the attachment of many summers to controlling Mother, and scene of the labors of the German maid Anna, thought of during so many nights. Evidently I was not yet the free man I so proudly thought of myself as being.

The first night was indicative that the world is never one hundred percent lost. My mind set on the pleasures of the body, a cosy wood fire warming the master bedroom, we received an unexpected visit from a sister-in-law. She sat on the bed and told us at some length that Anna, that same maid, had had a hysterical attack that day! It seemed a long time before we had ourselves to ourselves.

Early June can be cool in Connecticut—with frequent rains. There was the clay tennis court to get into shape; long walks through the damp brush; meals to fix; I suppose movies in town. It wasn't exciting, though I was excited by it.

I found myself often strumming at the piano, an emptiness in heart at ignorance of where the thoughts of that young girl, my wife, might be. Constant openness has to be a decision; it's not automatic.

We went on gratefully to arrangements where painting could once again be the center for me.

The next year a lengthy trip together to Europe and all the museums and art cities was the real honeymoon. We found love and happiness in a mutual enjoyment of it all.

Yet the Not-OK elements in our scripts and life positions were already preparing other things.

Art Abandoned

We had rented a new apartment in London Terrace on

West 23rd Street for our first married year. There I painted portraits of Norris and brought in models to pose, not in the nude, but for portrait studies. Somehow it wasn't a satisfying life for her and earlier dreams began to revive.

Her largely dominated and unhappy childhood had had wonderful breaks in it when she visited her Aunt Fan and Uncle George on the farm in Virginia. They were loving and indulgent and poured out positive strokes to a little girl in a background of rural abundance.

What matter that the old house was a bit tumble-down, that cash income was not great! There were chickens around the door, neighboring children to play with, a horse to ride, trips to the store, much visiting around and endless easy conversation over generous meals. A paradise of nurtured life contrasted to the negative strokes at home.

So a script pattern was formed for her: *if you're not happy, get back to the farm.* What more natural than that it would make a better life for the young Mitchell Binghams!

I believe it was in Miami, in the sun, where we were enjoying the scene of my own childhood happinesses on a visit, that she proposed that we take up farming together.

Many men may have some tie to the land—the thought of working hard physically and producing actual food rather than illusions—the out-of-doors, which by that time I had learned to love. It didn't seem as big a change as it actually was.

Hooked by the sex we were having, wanting to please the fair lady who was providing it, in no way tied to a job for income, I was being the man I wanted to show I was—in sex. Now let me be a man also in work and earning money. I had no idea whether such was possible.

So I readily agreed to give up the career in which I had invested so much time and passion already for an unknown hope mostly held by my new wife.

Looking back I'm surprised at this decision myself. What I see is that the strokes I was getting were real and assured—art had been a starvation form of self-stroking—and with little or no experience of getting along with another person except under duress, I assumed the way to assure a constant supply of strokes was to do what the other person wanted. Thus I tied myself to a dependency.

Europe Again

Once the decision made that I would switch careers, take some courses in agriculture and move to Salem, where I already had a house and studio waiting—it had been given by that same fairy grandmother—there seemed no great hurry to implement it. Norris had established her role; we could go to Europe.

We set off in the fall in the years when Fascism and Naziism were reaching their apogee, still blissfully unaware that this world was not a cherry put there for our biting.

It turned out to be a cold winter. As a boy I had travelled Europe in hot summers and was used to luxurious museum visits. As a student in Montmartre, I had sat on the radiator to keep warm, but had forgotten it.

The Medici Chapel in Florence was beautiful as ever but the icy glare of marble divinities reached our marrow! In Venice a gondola has to float on water and the Adriatic is partly at least glacier fed. We sniffled and found no comfort.

Finally, in desperation, we headed for modernism in the mountains. Sestrières was a ski resort on the frontier above Turin. A round hotel tower rose from the snow with adequate heat.

Vigorous exercise all day among the glorious slopes—we were both novices—soon restored our health and better spirits.

Had I but known it, there in a microcosm was presented the history to come. Columns of uniformed Italians practiced skiing all day by themselves, bolstering the Alpini regiments. Our instructors were blond, skillful Austrians, who, like demi-gods, not only laughed at my awkwardness—I hadn't outlived that script injunction—but in some subtle way showed that the master race would use and tolerate but never treat as equals the Mediterraneans in whose lands they were.

I gathered these impressions half consciously and with some

surprise—of course unaware of what they foreshadowed. As an American, I had always roamed the world superior because equality is best and money paves the way.

Norris and I had a happy Christmas to ourselves—little candles on the window sill. In my mind and muscles I was stretching for the farm.

The Physical Farm

In considering the twelve years spent on the farm, years when the world was exploding around us but which were comparatively peaceful for me, I must divide my life into two different aspects, the physical and the spiritual or psychic. Though this is primarily a psychic history, it behooves me to mention the physical side as frame for what was happening within.

Aside from an attack of jaundice at the beginning, seeming to stem from overwork and anxiety, as I rushed at the things to be done, these were magnificent years of health and strength. Forgotten were competition of body and thus awkwardness; there was no need for agility or excess muscle, but mere persistence in arduous tasks that needed to be learned.

I was never, I felt, very good at milking, which required a *feel* for the udder, but my companions never complained. In handling tools I developed simple skills and quite proudly, when off in the fields with my tractor I made the repairs as needed.

The inside work was long and not much loved, though the smells of hay, grain and silage in the dusty old barn remain as odorous and delicious reminders.

Out in the fields, on the other hand, with the sun and air I savored every moment—every view a joy as the trees on the sides of the fields, the delicate waves of the hills, even the pond, often seen, bordered the rich combination of loam, grass, tall corn or even tangled soybeans, upon which we carried on our agronomic operations.

In later discussions with members of the family as to whether I was happy in those years, they refer as follows: "But you were always singing on the tractor. We could hear you all over the farm." Truly it was so. Free Child must have carried on from the summers of childhood, revelling in out-of-doors awareness—the world beyond the Salem valley happily put aside.

There may have even been an element of the *"I'll Show You"* in it. A man who sings or whistles has an audience, if only imaginary. It could be I was loudly proclaiming: "You see I can after all. I'm happily married. I've learned to work."

Mine Is Better Than Yours

However, in other respects those years on the farm were not so idyllic and the psychic aspects are perhaps more interesting to contemplate.

Thomas Harris, author of *I'm OK—You're OK,* sets forth the hypothesis that the basic game people play which springs from the Not-OK positions is "Mine Is Better Than Yours." This seems indeed more like activity to gain the Vengeful position I'm OK—You're Not OK than a game which requires a responder.

Be that as it may, when engaged in art I had assumed my own talent and fantasized over recognition to come, even if, as in Vermeer's case, it came after 200 years. I hadn't worried too much about others in the field as I was calmly superior about most contemporary work I saw.

After a cursory look at an expensive farm in New Jersey, suggested by Dr. Brill, we had easily decided to settle in Salem, where the land was already available, a dairy farm was in operation, and my Granny's agent, Cousin Don, was voicing the desire to hand over responsibility to some family member.

Skipping for the moment over the ups and downs necessary to get started, some horrendous and some humorous mistakes of judgment chargeable to naiveté and inexperience, a few years saw me installed as head of a large operation of 75 milking cows and 30 young stock, 300 acres under cultivation, 6 or 7 men employed, including a genial character as Yankee foreman who knew all I didn't know.

I studied hard, tested and kept endless records, taught myself double-entry bookkeeping, put in capital of my own and persuaded my brothers to allow lumber to be sold so their capital could also be harvested.

Connecticut farming was and is in a decline; the small patches of open fields under cultivation in the overall woodland grow smaller each year. Ours was one of the few large herds in the county. Facing losses every year but one, I was determined it become the most profitable if not the biggest. (I thought often of outdoing a Scotchman named Mackenzie, our closest competitor, yet whom as a man I hardly knew.)

When after a decade of struggle and sweat I saw the losses continue and faced like Sisyphus a never-ending uphill fight, I became discouraged and decided I didn't want that for the rest of my life.

Norris, who had enjoyed a smaller operation around our own house, along with bearing and raising our three children, was alarmed and said: "Why don't we cut down the size to a one-or-two family farm that we can manage without such strain?" I tried it—we sold off the main herd and kept a few choice animals and kept one good friend as employee.

But it was bitter ashes in my mouth. The dream of biggest and best which had sustained the output of energy all those years was gone. Where for Norris the dream was based on childhood charm, my hope was shattered. And soon I announced I was quitting it entirely and going back to the arts I loved.

My theory is that Mine Is Better Than Yours is what I do when I'm not doing what deep in my heart I really want. If I listen to the creative Little Professor which, after all is part of Free Child, then I can be easy about others. But if I'm in the grip of one of the Not-OK counterscript drivers which operate in Adaptive Child, such as Please Me (in this case Please Norris) or Try Hard or Be Strong, then indeed I am more apt to want the recognition strokes of doing better than others. I measure myself against them.

The Harrises say we play that game "to bring a little momentary relief from the awful burden of the Not OK." As we've seen in the introduction, Taibi Kahler, able developer of the "Miniscript," describes how the counterscript drivers get us into Not OKness. By contrast, the OK Allowers as shown by the sympathetic Hedges Capers basically proclaim: It's OK to be yourself and do your own thing.

I thank God I decided to quit when I did. The Explorer was ready to move on. In any case, my script is more Tantalus than Sisyphus. I'm not so interested in rolling the same stone up the same hill all my life and having it roll down, as I am in moving on to ever-new bunches of grapes which may dangle out of reach, or stooping to drink from fresh new pools which may or may not dry up as I approach.

Equality—Employees

Our first summer in Salem, after the farming decision, had been spent by Norris and myself growing great quantities of beets and Brussels sprouts without the least idea how properly to pack or market them. I soon also started driving three times a week many miles over the hills to the state agricultural college to take some basic courses in agronomy, nutrition and genetics.

For the first years of the dairy I contented myself with learning and supervising at the same time. But the same Parent pressure which had driven my mother to a simple structure for her country house and led me to an attic fifth-floor walk-up my first year in Paris in the worker's quarter, insisted on equality with all men whether employed by me or not, and led to the fairly drastic step of learning and doing all the different chores that my men did. I didn't want to be the "gentleman farmer" that in reality I was. Parent clearly was pressing on me with the following dicta: "Don't ask anyone to do what you can't do yourself" and "You can't be equal with them if you don't dirty your hands in the same way."

I realize equality may not be a philosophically tenable concept. That doesn't mean I couldn't vigorously seek it.

Throughout the years I kept trying to perfect a share-the-profits scheme. One of the younger men asked: "What will be in it for us?", which was realistic in that there were no profits to divide!

The basic problem to which I had no answer was that there was dissension and rivalry among the men. Even though Bill Maynard, the shrewd old Yankee who exercised much of the real power of management, brought in a nephew and a son-in-law, family relationship didn't prevent bad feeling and unpleasant remarks.

Later, when with Moral Re-Armament I had supposedly found an answer to universal division through change, I used to say: "The trouble with the farm was that I had no answer to help the men get along." However, now I am clear they mostly all worked well and skillfully. And I'm more inclined to lay the failure to simple inefficiency of the old structures which demanded massive extra labor and the general unsuitability of the rich but rocky Connecticut soil—especially near big cities in war time, where wages had to be high.

A more complex problem is how I could be competitive in terms of the biggest and best farm in the county and yet not enjoy nor expect extra privilege vis-à-vis the men. I believe TA offers the simplest explanation in terms of the Drivers.

Our own farm was our own group as a family is. Within that my Driver would be what it had been with Mother and was being with Norris, i.e., Please Me (Please Them) and mixed with that Be Perfect—"Don't be superior or take advantage of." Others were the outgroup, whom I didn't know and whom I could excel—the outgroup about whom we had been told as children: The Bingham brothers are better than anybody else.

Individually I liked the men and even Ken Hill, the son-in-law who was not fond of me, I tried to please and give strokes to without knowing how. The implication that it would have made the farm run better had I known more about stroking is a materialistic one. It might be true but friendship must be a reward in itself—strokes are needed for themselves and mustn't be traded for results in other endeavors. My desire for power wanted success and could later blame those in whom Parent could find some fault for not attaining it.

Towards the end of the farm episode, I pressed the issue of

equal pay beyond what Bill Maynard had set up by equalizing the wages for the outside day help regardless of how long they had been with us or how skillful they were. I antagonized the best and this I now regret. It was a typical Parent-Knows-Best decision, not based on human sympathies but on theory. How like the moralistic way in which our country has often handled other nations!

Servants

Norris didn't have the same Parent-inspired attitude towards employees as I did. And since she took the lead in decisions involving both of us, the years on the farm saw us with a series of domestics in the home, to which if they could be obtained she saw no objection.

Role playing was more or less taken for granted with us in those years. That is I, the husband, might have the say in the business outside the house. It was equally natural for her, the wife, to have the say in matters concerning the home. I was pleased to go along.

In these latter days when domestics seem a luxury only for the super rich, it's nostalgic and may be worthwhile to give a few words on each, so different they were. We had added a back wing to the house for the very purpose of private quarters for them.

The first was Mrs. Hersey, a motherly woman who took us, the inexperienced couple, under her wing and specialized in catch-all soups and stews, "There's everything good in it!"

Next, a black couple, at the time Nat was born, showed interesting differences, as the wife took on cooking, laundering and much real care for the baby, while the husband, as butler, gleamed in a white coat as he opened the door for me fresh from the barn with its smells.

Another white couple had been hired, with the wife only working, while the husband, a skilled retired carpenter, was to enjoy residence. This wound up with bad feelings, as he undertook making fine kitchen cabinets and so on without adequate clarification of arrangements; we ended up by paying unexpected union rates.

During the war years we had a couple of whom the husband was Japanese, a trained chef who not only prepared sumptuous dishes but made exquisite miniature gardens and water colors, while his wife, a New England-born brunette, fussed over restrictions imposed on citizens of "enemy" origin in wartime. Every time we went out, he would invade the yard, and soon stone lanterns, little arched bridges, and pools were transforming it into a reflection of Oriental culture. This courteous gentleman, whose wife had since died, reappeared briefly in Miami years later.

None of these I've mentioned stayed many years in what to them must have seemed deep country—fifteen miles from New London.

Eventually we secured, less artificially, the help of a capable local woman, Pearl Daniels, who, with a husband and two robust sons in her own home, managed to take us to her heart. Her especial darling was our daughter Lucy. Norris had been maturing all these years and was able to attain an intimacy with Pearl that she might not have done as a newly-married girl. Pearl gave of herself in countless strokes as one of the family.

Friends

I wrote earlier that I left our social contacts mostly in Norris's hands. And I also wrote that friendships which are for giving and receiving strokes must be their own reward.

How did we do through those years in this area? And what did it do or not do for me, especially in view of the paucity of friendships I had had before Norris came along?

We met and made friends with several but not many establishment couples of our own age group. They were enough to give a solid basis of social life for Norris. We often exchanged small dinners in each other's homes at which I assisted and was pleasantly tolerated. Not being a golfer, hunter or much of a drinker, I didn't get separately into any men's groups. I joined a club in New London but never went—the script command: *Be Shy,* was too powerful for that.

It's clear I only came out under Norris's wing and thus took a powerless position which could turn to Victim at any new turn of events. Norris knew this and rarely let me forget it.

However, my stroke life was much richer than in the lonely European wanderings, business took energy and thought, life itself provided a wider base of contacts.

Fuller Potter and his girlwife, from the Tennessee mountains; Steve Brosnatch (now Steve Wheeler), a New York art friend; and during the war years a number of members of the British merchant marine, who were threading submarine-infested waters, on rest leave, all added variety and spice to our relationships.

After the news came out that our marriage was exploding in divorce, one of the establishment husbands that we knew told Norris that he'd be happy to set her up in an apartment. She promptly told me. I was staggered that our friendship was so shallow that it would give way to that so quickly. In Eric Berne's description of the Kick-Me player he quotes the typical player as saying piteously after the kick: "Why does this always happen to me?" The deep truth is that I had never evaluated the gentleman through my own intuition but only through Norris's eyes. And probably in his own eyes he was quite restrained to wait until it was clear we were parting.

More recently I feel more solidly entrenched in my various friendships, because I know how to give positive strokes and want to—I like people. The return becomes less necessary. And perhaps equally important I rate the strokes I do get more precisely and look for more specific ones rather than kind generalities. We reach closer to intimacy.

Bulls and Nightmares

A dark side to the farm life which I discussed with no one was what had happened to the fear which had been such a cloud in earlier years. The pleasures of intercourse with a complaisant wife and a richer social exchange may have funneled off much of the psychic energy which once went into negative. And what quarrels Norris and I did have usually wound up with me in Victim position, a peculiar Not-OKness whose feeling I can recall exactly.

Our men, headed by Bill Maynard, were fairly rough in handling the cows, shouting and knocking them about the face when any driving was to be done. When I began farming, a bull was always kept in an indoor pen and only visited when the cows were in heat.

But as we began to raise our own replacements, to test cows for their production and keep careful pedigrees, we had to obtain more than one valuable bull, after careful study of his ancestry. In line with approved practice, exercise yards were built for these animals and breeding stalls, which supposedly eliminated danger in handling. I knew that every once in a while farmers were killed by supposedly tame bulls. One especially of our fancier ones was named "Dictator," and in constant fury, pounding the stout oak planks of his pen, lived up to that name. Occasionally one of the bulls would escape, and when it was "Dictator," roaming the roads with fire in his eye, the men lined up with staves and drove him to his quarters.

I observed these proceedings from a distance. I was afraid, and I hated that fear, which hurt my pride. We never discussed it.

But just as in earlier years my recurring dream had been that I was back in school, collecting the negative strokes inherent for me in that dominated situation, so for twenty years after Salem a recurring dream would be that I was chased by a bull.

Hedges Capers and Glenn Holland write in the *TA Journal* of a stroke quotient which each of us needs for survival, and that if we don't get the positive—not knowing how—we'll automatically collect the negative. And it seems that with my conscious life desperately turned toward success and the positive, yet not free of negative addiction, dreamtime was my time for building up that negative stock. I was unaware that the very loathing with which I underwent these repeated assaults in dreams would reinforce their qualification as secretly needed.

I'll have more to say of these dreams later on.

War Measures and Organizations

Salem was then a community of some six to eight hundred souls—it's now over a thousand, organized into a "Township," which in New England traditionally retains a lot of self-governing power and is close to pure democracy. I was to take part in various organizations during my years there and learn a lot about how they function. This was usually done at meetings which took me away from home in the evenings. I don't remember Norris ever complaining at this if she felt it. It probably built up gradually.

During the war organizations proliferated especially. I suppose humanity had to do something about this horror it was perpetrating on itself. Each group could channel and release some of the energy generated.

For example, we were receiving glowing reports of the heroic efforts of the Londoners during the Blitz. Some official conceived the idea we should use their methods in readiness for air attacks. "Air raid wardens" were organized in both town and country. As a patriot I had to join!

A practice blackout was scheduled. All lights were turned out or windows blackened. In the pitch dark I went out on the country road and walked up and down, guided by faint starlight between the trees. It was fun. But if a car with no lights had come along—God knows how!—it might have been dangerous. It was nonsense and I resigned, but some murmured that that was not patriotic!

At the same time, in each town airplane spotting crews were arranged and towers built to identify approaching craft. Once every so often my friend and employee, Wallace Maynard, and I would take on the "graveyard" shift, from midnight till four in the morning. We would try to stay awake with thermoses of coffee. There were elaborate instructions for reporting.

Only once during the entire duration of this program did an aeroplane actually come into view. And then we were far too excited to report it accurately!

Lest you think all our activities were quite so useless, let me give a quick list of the groups I was part of in those years and the positions I held. In Salem if you began and became known for it, there was little restraint in enlisting you in each one. Thus: organizer of forest firefighting crew; charter member and treasurer, Salem Volunteer Fire Company; trustee and treasurer, Salem Library; chairman Salem Rationing Board; member Salem Board of Education; member Salem Board of Selectmen. That seems enough to remember for now.

I might add that a county-wide Selective Service board had informed me that production of food was essential, that I was not only too old for the Armed Services but should definitely continue such valuable doings as farming.

My late twenties and thirties were thus vigorously active years for me, with many strokes coming in. Quietly but more importantly, however, a whole new phase of life was coming into unexpected focus. Parenthood was to bring fundamental changes.

Nat

We decided to have a child, as I suppose many people do, without any idea of what that would entail.

I was busy but strong—the failure of the farm venture was still many years away—and seemed well settled into activity. Our house had been generously remodeled; we had domestics helping out at home. Norris was flourishing with the outdoor life. Families in general have children. So why not?

With all I'd been through in my own childhood and a vague decision that I wouldn't do as my parents did or be like them, I never thought of all that needs to be given positively, the care, attention and concern so that my life will no longer belong to me as much as before. It would be fun, another adventure.

The first hurricane to hit Connecticut in over a hundred

years, the famous one of 1938, disrupted the amenities that autumn for several weeks. In spite of lack of electricity, having to carry our water in buckets, and no telephone, the pregnancy proceeded normally. Nathaniel Shaw, whom we were to call Nat, a bouncing boy, arrived in the New London hospital November 15th, after I had wearied and gone home for the night—indication of the selfishness which motivated me fundamentally through those years.

We did all that was physically necessary, guided by a pediatrician and the universal Dr. Spock. Feedings at all hours; we even installed a microphone in his room so that we could hear every cry. As we went on, two things didn't quite seem like the books.

One, he would go to sleep over the bottle and have to be patted strenuously to encourage finishing the requisite amount. And soon he began to rock back and forth in the crib, till finally it would travel across the room and have to be nailed down. This puzzled us completely.

We were neither battering nor hostile parents. But we hadn't heard of strokes and somehow reserved most of the fondling for each other. Photos of those years show a loving mother and even a loving father, but it's easy to feel benevolent for the birdie. It's not true that all parents nurture naturally as much as is needed, especially when they've been preoccupied in youth with their own needs and problems.

How to Obtain Strokes

You'll remember that my nightmares seem to have been prompted by the need, unfulfilled during the busy days, of negative strokes, i.e., strokes which *feel bad.*

Nat, so far as I know, didn't go in for bad dreams or passive reactions. As I said, we weren't hostile but equally bad we were unloving. So to survive, he had to develop methods of stroking himself or of getting strokes.

The ferocious rocking in the crib, which involves the whole

body, is obviously a strong form of self-stroking. The energy Nat put into this has carried over in a remarkable way into his adult life. He takes on difficult, rugged work—he's now a fisherman on the cold Pacific coast—and enjoys overcoming the resistance of nature in the wild.

Getting strokes from others, the other need fulfilled, was based on simple experience. If you go to sleep, i.e., resist your physical need for food on a schedule, you'll be given strokes—vigorous pats they were—and get the food besides. So resist even if the strokes you get aren't the pleasantest; they will come.

I'm reminded of my own rebellious sleeps. However, my rebellions have a passive quality based, as I suggest, on an Alice image and not daring to speak out.

Nat's were more active, I'm glad to say, though at the time they drove us "up the wall." He soon evolved a more efficient method of getting intense attention than going to sleep. After solid food began to replace milk, he would hold it in his cheek and refuse to swallow what he didn't like. Long contests of will took place in which Nat was an easy winner, Norris the principal loser and I an uneasy and puzzled second loser. He was the victor because he got both much recognition for being difficult and survived physically. We couldn't ignore this or put him on one side.

The Pen and Angry Reactions

However, as he got older, we retaliated. Playpens are common for leaving babies in where they can play and exercise all at once. Why not build a bigger one which would give more room and be safer out of doors? So Tony, the Polish handyman who had made many of the improvements on our place, was again pressed into service. A great structure of floor and columns like the Parthenon emerged. It was a better prison but still a prison.

As we went off for some errand or other, Nat would peer through the bars at us and give them a shake.

He was a child with a nice dimple on the chin and an attractive smile when it came; others found him easily lovable. Perpetually curious, he would enter a room and immediately try every knob and handle in sight.

For me it wasn't just indifference or neglect.

I would observe him and get strong reactions. During his childhood and with a powerful background of what I felt was Freudian insight, I could pick out self-centered behaviour and condemn it silently. Then, when it went too far, either endangering himself or the comfort of others, I could burst out in indignant punishment and feel justified in doing so. At present I see this as coming from the Critical Parent ego state which I now hate in myself as well as in others. But at the time, in spite of an uncomfortable turbulence inside, I never felt such outbursts were not excusable. Wasn't he the one who was behaving badly?

Just as I had collected brown stamps at school which were to vindicate rebellious outbreaks, so I collected brown stamps watching Nat and then felt justified in angry scolding or spanking. During my own childhood I had been completely sold on the proposition: *Though it's wrong any other time, anger is OK if you're in Parent.*

A miraculous footnote to this is to record that Nat himself shows no such tendency today. With his own daughter he's a model of endless patience. I breathe a prayer of thanksgiving that the Critical Parent state is one he doesn't seem to get himself into.

This issue came up a few years later in terms of Russell, our second son. But change was to begin much sooner than that.

CHAPTER SIX

A New Element Introduced

Nurturing Parent

One day when Nat was already five, Norris came to me and introduced what was to be a whole new concept of life. She had taken him around to various specialists and experts in child care, including the Gesell Institute in New Haven. They had all examined him thoroughly and found nothing wrong. Various suggestions had been made which didn't seem to mean anything specific.

Whether out of the blue, out of her Little Professor, out of the Spirit of the Almighty, or out of the deep wisdom within, she said a simple thing which was to prove revolutionary in my life: *"You know the real trouble is we haven't loved him enough."*

I can't pretend that I saw all at once how profound this was or what consequences it would bring. But I did accept it. The consequences are still flowing.

I knew it meant change. A new mountain range had risen out of the mists, it would be necessary to see what lay on the other side.

Nat's behaviour was puzzling. I would try to restore for the past and develop a new attitude. Any more children would be truly loved right from the start. Sure enough, when Russell came in the fall of 1944 and Lucy in December 1946, we were ready and strokes of appreciation and love went their way immediately and from then on.

I had never heard of Nurturing Parent. I knew mainly of my resentments against my own parents, which I had hashed out so thoroughly in psychoanalysis. But hidden behind those negatives was the positive model of the big self-consciously smiling man, my father, who had given encouragement in so many ways and somehow of whose care I had been aware through the fear, without wanting to admit it. Nurturing Parent existed in my head and was about to take charge sometimes of my action. I've had to learn what it means, but I've never gone back on the decision or stopped listening to what Nurturing Parent had to say.

No Sinecure

This change has been slow; it has taken time to grow from one stage to another. There have been failures and slipbacks. Don't think it came all at once and was over and done with, as easily as it takes to say it or to read about it.

For example, though I accepted Norris's word and saw it as true, we didn't have much idea how to implement it with Nat. By the time he was seven or eight we had sent him to a prepreparatory boarding school and when that didn't work out, he went to a little family-style rustic school called "Fireside," where he was cherished and seemed to get on well.

After that, and following what seemed a scientific and experimental bent, he went on to Putney School in Vermont, where various "advanced" educational methods were being worked out.

Nat learned a stoicism similar to my own, where discomfort and hardship are concerned. The Be Strong driver: Don't show it if something's wrong; it won't do any good—led him through these changing schools, unable to tell us what he really felt. How, for instance, he had hated the first one when he was really young.

I've told you many things of my own life which weren't easy, where shame is hot. But there are none which I feel more keenly than this shuffling of responsibility after an answer has begun to come. I believe Norris was the prime mover in these sendings-away, she found Nat too difficult and it was easy to imagine other teachers would be preferable. But I went along without a murmur, determined to improve with the other children, and thus refusing to pay the price of the past.

Nat is exquisitely forgiving and thus it's hard to say: This or that would have worked out better. I cannot maintain, however, that a wrong is not a wrong because the sufferer has risen above the damage it did.

Nat is our child. Once a child knows who his parents are and has made the basic decisions of his script, if then they decide they've been wrong with him, it would seem best for them and for him to get a chance to work it out together. As it was, we prepared to skim the cream of the new decisions with love for Russell and Lucy and to let Nat fight it out by himself.

Psychosomatics

During the years after the war, various of my brothers began coming back to Connecticut and Salem from their assignments in the services. Charles, or Carlo as we nicknamed him, the middle brother of the seven, was a doctor who practiced medicine and owned property in Hartford. We had seen him and his wife often in the earlier years when their children were small, when we drove up there for visits.

He now became more important in my life as he began to specialize in and preach psychosomatic medicine. I seized on this amplification and extension of the action of the subconscious, which Charles saw as generally applicable in every bodily ill.

Norris was the principal sufferer from this conversion as far as I was concerned. She had an ordinary number of complaints. And I could thus get into Parent and grandly diagnose what was wrong with her spirit. Being Victim in some arguments, as I've said, I was usually Persecutor about money and now could be complacent Persecutor whenever she had a cold or a headache.

Later in the divorce action, when she brought "mental cruelty" as the offense, she was to use these analyses of mine and rightly so. It must have been insufferable to have the misery doubled at every slight disorder.

I won't try to give the rationale of this idea system here, or to amplify it in exposition. Almost every one of us has a viewpoint and accepts some psychosomatic explanations of certain ills, while rejecting others. Carlo, as I say, tended to go the whole way. Within a few years I was to undertake with him the writing and illustration of a booklet enlarging on this theme.

What seems hardly credible and yet is so human after all in its pursuit of the "Mine Is Better Than Yours" is the almost total disregard of how these ideas would affect the poor person on whom they were inflicted, true or not. While Norris was the main victim from me, Charles in more complete stubbornness insisted on their application in every situation.

He had been an attractive and popular young man. As a couple, he and Kathleen belonged to the upper-middle-class smart set. So he had obtained several good positions and responsibilities as well as a fair practice. But colleagues of more conservative view were outraged to be called out-of-date on every problem and soon he was asked to resign from the jobs. Before many years he had given up his practice as well.

I see in this for me, as well as for him, that we have been what Eric Berne calls "hard" players of the "Kick Me" game. Ignoring the response I'm likely to get from a contradicting disagreement is not just due to ignorance or stupidity; my intuition is too clever for that. It is a deliberate provocation from the subconscious whose aim is the very negative stroke that I end up getting—all in the name of the "truth"!

Others with the same "true" material but a more winning script will know how to manage it in small enough doses to retain acceptability.

Thus, just as Carlo had out of the Karpman Triangle and a use of the Persecutor position, I was able in the long run to gain my preferred position of Victim again. Time was beginning to run out on the marriage.

Sex

I drew a partial veil on the pleasant sex activities of the early years with Norris. Let me say that what weaknesses there had been in those years became sharpened and more important as the marriage reached the stage of crisis and dissolution.

There was no slackening of my desire for it and I believed in my love for her. The greater importance of love that had come with the experience with Nat and reached full flower with Russell and Lucy didn't cleanse or cure the increasingly sharp clashes that sent us back and forth from Persecutor to Victim or vice versa.

She wouldn't believe in my love. Constant premature ejaculations, for that is what it became, persuaded her that I was bluffing and didn't really care. Neither of us saw at that time the lure of the negative, the thrill of the Kick Me game. For me these episodes were painful. I would keep on promising a better result next time, which I suppose is characteristic of a good game player. The conscious will was all in the Please Me driver (Please Norris) and Be Perfect. Only at a deeper level was the script injunction: *You will never attain* gaining more and more command.

Norris has told me of how painful for her was the decision to give up farming and the farm. Although at the time she accepted with seeming grace the resolve to buy a small trailer and head for Florida, underneath it broke the back of our marriage.

And this, though I sought sex with her as anxiously as ever. In her spirit she began to look for an out.

I have a hunch, though of course I can't prove it, that had I stuck with the farm, she would have stuck with me, insufficient as this basis obviously was. So often there is the balance of negative strokes in games that couples play with one another that they are kept together by these rewards. By seeking a different dynamic of forces I unwittingly released her to seek a different dynamic also.

It's of interest that of us seven brothers I'm still the only one to go through the chasm of divorce.

Florida

So we went to Florida, the first year for a few months only, but after that for longer times. It was to become my base for more than twenty-five years, though interrupted by much travel. As Norris had sought the farm, so, I believe, I sought in the land where I'd been happiest as a child, a recrudescence and continuation of that pleasure.

As a baby, Lucy was bright-eyed and curious almost from birth. But she began to suffer from asthmatic attacks. The doctor recommended the South, where the air was warm, if we didn't want to keep her in hospitals all winter. This provided a legitimate reason to pull up some of our stakes and at least give it a try in south Florida, a hospitable region we already knew.

Granny had died ten years before—leaving me and all her grandsons independent. This, of course, I cherished, and in spite of the drain of the farm business, I never allowed it to disappear.

Mother and her second husband, Henry Gregor, lived on the same property on Brickell Avenue in Miami and would welcome a visit.

January 1947—the Connecticut ground was covered with heavy snow as we, Russell, Lucy, Norris and myself (Nat was in school), started off with the new rig—an eighteen-foot house on wheels, with all the little conveniences which delight campers and travelers.

The trip was full of ups and downs and adventure. An accident on the ice gave excitement and delay. Norris was intrigued enough by the unaccustomed episodes to write them up afterwards in colorful style.

We had long stays with Mother and Henry, and also trips further south to the Everglades and the Keys, with their shimmering beaches. We made many friends with genial spirits, some also fleeing from northern rigors and the restraints of their working lives.

Would paradise prove itself to be paradise?

The World—Back to the Arts

I believe in each of us is a real or potential concern for the world and what happens in it. Many feel they have to stifle this because of the difficulties of their own survival—they become just too busy. Others, grieving over the hardships of their early lives and heeding the Parent teaching: "Life is tough; you can't trust anybody," decide for cynicism and discount that care for humanity in themselves.

Describing the difficulty, Paul Campbell, physician to and follower for many years of Dr. Frank Buchman, founder of Moral Re-Armament, in a fundamental address given in 1968 says: "Man tends to smallness." This smallness, the negative energy that he posits, is, of course, the enemy of the solicitude for humanity which I am advancing.

War with its patriotic appeal to everyone in the nation relies on the positive élan—the successful wars being backed by the faith of the majority that somehow their battle is answering a fundamental human need. In my time on the farm during World War II, I consoled myself that in helping to produce food I was doing my bit in the struggle against totalitarian dictatorships. I don't believe anyone could live through a war like that in which their own country was involved without establishing some connection to having a part, except those so absorbed in destructive Not-Ok scripts that that voice would be drowned out.

In my early years with art in Europe and New York I *was* too self-centered, too "small," to listen to any larger interest, whether present in my head or not. But as an adult, having lived vicariously through the battles of France and Britain, Pearl Harbor, the Pacific, and the final holocausts of Hiroshima and Nagasaki, I couldn't return to that smallness without a continued link to the world.

Creativity in the arts was beckoning once more; the world of business had been too unrewarding. I had begun to wonder whether I couldn't achieve with pen and typewriter the recognition—strokes from others—that I had failed at with brush and palette, much as I loved those tools. So in line with my father's model of exploration, I risked embarking on a new venture and actually produced the manuscript of a novel.

Its background theme, appositely enough, was the regeneration of man through change in the midst of the nuclear destruction of the old society. Thus extraordinarily the growth that had begun to come to me through the love in Nurturing Parent was reaching out already in fiction for concrete betterment of the race. It was the same that was to bring me a few years later to join an organization dedicated to that end, namely: Moral Re-Armament.

However, some dark hours would intervene between the one and the other, between fantasy and membership.

The Beaches

It was agreeable to sit in the sun on a sandy beach sheltered from the wind, a few yards away from the baby sleeping in a crib. She was gaining strength; I was able to scribble away on my novel.

One day, after we had found an idyllic spot down on the Keys, I was sitting thus in a beach chair in shorts and not much else, writing under an umbrella with the hot sun blazing down. No one else was near.

A Cadillac drew up along the simple track. An important man with a cigar got out and looked around, followed by two gaudily beflowered ladies. He looked me over and then asked: "What are you? Some kind of beachcomber or something?" I was delighted.

After the manuscript was finished and I had initiated a few desultory and unconvinced moves to get it out to the world, I went back to the safer ground of my early love, art.

Perhaps if I had by that time really thought seriously of the world, I would have pushed my book somewhat harder. But the idea of saving mankind had been expressed in the story. That done, I wanted instant recognition or enthusiasm. If not, I would assume I wasn't a writer, couldn't write well (Oh—the Be Perfect Driver!) and take up something I felt I could do: paint paintings. I would make them small, price them low and see if those wouldn't achieve at least a few positive strokes.

Now that Norris was no longer lavishing many of those, unconsciously aware of the need for them—we were still sleeping together—I was beginning to sink from the quadrant of I'm OK—You're Not OK (I'll show you I can!) to a desperation: "I'm Not OK and I don't know who is. Does no one want me or appreciate my efforts?"

The landscapes produced in that period show a certain quality and as always I feasted on the beauty of nature, here the color of the tropics "where every prospect pleases . . . "

Thinking of Gauguin, Robert Louis Stevenson, Van Gogh and many others, as well as myself, it seems as if seeking a paradise is often one of the despairing last moves in a "hard" game. Soon we find complete breakdown—either death, divorce, or some other break.

Korea—Fishing

While I was trying to live, the world went on its larger way subject to mighty forces which, while coming from the same human sources as my actions and reactions, were multiplied a millionfold by those who exercised power in the so-called supernations. Hopefully the war was over. But Korea burst forth and reminded us that we weren't so free.

I no longer had milk production as an oblation to put on the altar of national service. Even at best making or selling landscapes of the enchanting Florida isles couldn't be made to seem very helpful. I applied to some of the huge organizations like the Friends Service Committee and the Red Cross to find no great eagerness for any assistance I might offer.

We had acquired some taste for the fishing available in those balmy waters. A wonderful couple whose roots were deep in southern land and water, Julian and Mary Kight, who sold bait from a colorful shack on the Gulf side of Long Key, encouraged this and helped me to buy a boat. Why not again put energy into food production, a task which could be done locally and yet add its mite to the resources of the nation?

I caught some fish. I went on a daring expedition with Julian across the Bay of Florida at night. There was no adequate shelter for the boat off the undeveloped shore of Long Key. The winds would come up strongly now from south, now from north. A titanic tide surged under the piers of Flagler's old mile-long bridge, now bearing the "highway across the sea."

Somehow despair haunted me more than ever. Looking back, I see the spectre of drowning was not far away in those blazing turquoise oceans.

But God had another plan. And, as I've said, suicide is not my ticket.

PART II

OK, YOU WIN

CHAPTER SEVEN

The New Faith

Change

Norris had told me she was interested in another man. This added to the I'm-Not-OK factors which weighed me down.

Like dry brush or leaves in spring, I needed a spark to rekindle the fires of life which at forty were capable of full excitement and energetic action.

The summer before, in 1950, Fuller Potter had taken me to an open AA (Alcoholics Anonymous) meeting. Though alcohol had never been my problem or game, I was impressed with the quality of honesty which I'd never met before. This stirred a hunger for the kind of environment in which I could be honestly myself, the kind I've discovered that group meetings offer and flourish under.

I had always made fun of Moral Re-Armament (MRA). Ruled as I was by Vengeful Child with an especial anti-church bias from the days at Groton, we knew about it as a family from the fact that brother Bruce had given it all his time for ten years already, and that Mother, grateful for their postwar care for the Germans, spent summers at Caux, the center in Switzerland, with her second husband, Henry Gregor.

But, feeling not so OK, looking desperately around for meaningful activity that would satisfy the Parent voice, "Be Useful," I found myself taking Nat up to Miami from Long Key to see an MRA play which was just then playing there to packed audiences of airline people.

Some time before, staying for a while at Mother's home on Brickell Avenue, I had chased one of the men of the group, who was also visiting her. He talked well. His name was Ray Purdy—he will come into the story more fully some ten years later. At that moment, however, I was determined to put him down, to prove him wrong. He was happy with Mother's interest and support and wasted little time on my arguments.

I suppose any change or switch is prepared in our hearts which reach out for the new, before our pride in consistency of the old is prepared to accept. All these things acting together had plowed the ground.

I wept all the way through that musical play, which was about two brothers—a bad one and a "good" self-righteous one. I saw myself in both. It was like a door opening!

I had been bad in that I had not done all that Parent wanted me to do, in that I had been rebellious. I had been self-righteous in the superiority to so many—They are Not OK!

Bruce was there, beaming, and afterwards graciously introduced me to many of his genial teammates. I was struck by the friendliness and care, but most of all by the reiterated words: "We need you." I, thrust out of her favor by Norris, unacceptable even as a volunteer in the larger non-profit endeavors, too old by far for the Armed Forces, I, whose services had never been rated very high by anybody, was needed! This was balm to the soul.

I would stick around and see what this was all about. They were doing something for the world.

Nat flew on the next day to school, thinking I knew not what.

Norris let me know she didn't need me back on the Keys, would welcome my finding something with which to occupy myself, though she, too, had joined in scoffing at the world-changers who let God tell them what to do.

George Fraser and Guidance

I began to see something of this crowd who were gathered in a "task force" of some hundreds from many nations to further industrial peace in the airlines, where they had already made considerable headway.

Two plays were being given. Meetings were held both within the group and out in the hangars and shops. These travelers were being given hospitality in some of the luxurious homes of Miami and suburbs like Coconut Grove and Coral Gables, where they held informal gatherings and made friends with their hosts.

I soon found occupation with my big station wagon, driving a carload from the theatre in the evenings after the show to their various homes and picking them up in the morning on their way to "team meetings." Here successful progress was reported, plans for the day were worked out, and so on. By attending these meetings and the plays, I was able to feed my curiosity about this remarkable group, the only ones I had yet seen who seemed dedicated to something other than their own situations.

Although I had met many the first two evenings with them, and Bruce was also staying at Brickell Avenue in Mother's guest cottage—by that time she had built herself a new home in Coral Gables—I soon gathered that apart from Bruce's friendship and closeness, a Scotch bachelor-musician named George Fraser was taking me on with many indications of care. He was the talented composer who had trained the active chorus and written many of their beautiful songs. He was a little man of wit and lively mind and seemingly shrewd knowledge of the human problems with which I had wrestled.

How I bathed already in the subtle and divine strokes that came from belonging and being cherished! The negative that had led me to try to down Ray Purdy in argument had vanished.

One evening some of us were gathered over cups at a coffeeshop table in earnest but light-hearted discussion. In the course of it I happened boastfully to lie: "I'm not afraid of anything!" (It was at least true that though obsessed with fear much of the time, I was willing to try things, my curiosity was great and I didn't shrink from new ideas.)

With his twinkle brighter than ever, George Fraser quickly replied: "In that case you won't mind writing down your thoughts, will you?"

Though I had long heard of "guidance," i.e., that Moral Re-Armament believed that God could speak to anyone who listened, that had been one of the principal sources of scepticism and merriment at their expense. My Protestantism, feeble as it was, had given to the Almighty a picture of much more dignified and other-worldly power than would condescend personally to whisper into my or any ordinary ear.

They had been so friendly lately, I had somehow forgotten the issue. This brought me up short; I was trapped. The force of change which had brought such copious tears during the plays was pressing me on. OK, I would try!

Provided with pen and paper, we each wrote down "whatever comes." After an interval it was suggested we "share," i.e., read to each other whatever had blossomed forth in the form of words.

No lights flashed or thunder rumbled. Whatever those first sentences, they were ordinary.

Nevertheless, thus began a practice from which I have never retreated in the twenty-five years since.

No longer confined just to MRA, those in many religious and metaphysical groups now practice "meditation" and proclaim its value. It has become respectable.

However, for me it has always meant writing the thoughts down—so that I can go on from one to another and not feel compelled to retain any new or difficult concepts in a treacherous memory. I call memory "treacherous" because even though it has well supplied this account, I often lose, for example, the latest dream.

And I soon made the decision to rise an hour early each day so that specific time would be made for this observance before breakfast. From this, too, I haven't receded, except once on a 4:00 A.M. trip from Lima over the Andes to Cuzco, the excitement was too much for the habit. Perhaps rising early to milk the cows, when I'd been on the farm, had helped so that the sacrifice wasn't as enormous for me as it seems to some.

For some weeks nothing remarkable appeared in what was written down. Looking back, the sentences seemed flowery and somewhat pious. I was already aware this was a group of "good" men and women and my usual conforming desire would dictate similar sweetness.

However, I was hearing a lot about "change" and the four standards of MRA. These were "absolute." Required were absolute honesty, absolute purity, absolute unselfishness and absolute love. Many stories were told of how bad behavior was improving and new good relationships were being established. It was suggested we "go over" these standards, i.e., measure our lives by them and see where we had fallen down and what needed putting right. Thus the Omniscient would tell us specifically how to change.

Sure enough, one day to my surprise, in the middle of generalities, I wrote down the words: "Apologize to your stepfather for never having loved him."

This was a revelation, as in the Bingham "well-brought-up" manner we were always nice to everybody and had accepted Henry Gregor, after our parents' divorce in 1935, with good grace and politeness. What I saw in a flash was that the flow of heart I had learned for the children must go more widely and that politeness was worth almost nothing if it concealed the hidden attitude: "My family background is better than yours."

I was giving this new life a whirl. Even though completely foreign to what had been my nature, I decided I might as well try carrying out the instruction.

First Atonement

Visiting Mother and Henry soon after, I asked to speak to him alone. He had inherited the use of Grandfather's huge carved table-desk. On the wall a plump Brahms reached for the keyboard. We faced each other.

In simple terms I explained my thought and said I was sorry

for the lack of love. He was polite and questioned me. Did my brothers feel the same way? I incautiously admitted that perhaps they did. This was something of which I had no proof and involved sharing other people's sins, which is not done. With further experience I learned carefully to avoid such a faux pas.

From that day I felt closer to Henry and assumed he felt the same. It gave a boost to my feeling that I was on the right track and that the Lord Himself had had a hand in this betterment of relations. An element which reinforced this belief was the very unexpectedness of the whole event.

Other restitutions were to come in due course.

As example, let me skip to the next summer. While living in Salem in the middle of what modest political activity I had attempted, I had come up against a big wheel of the town, Mike Urbanik, scion of one of the prominent Polish-Ukrainian families who had taken over cherishing of the rocky New England soil when many Yankees, lured by promise of western prairie gold, had moved on to easier lands. We had always maintained courteous relations; when small, Nat had been good friends with his son Philip. But I hadn't been happy over certain practices and had criticized him freely to others.

The thought came one morning: "Apologize to Mike for talking behind his back." This was hard! It was he who had done thus and so; my indignation had been righteous! I resisted and did nothing—I'm OK—He's Not OK dies hard. Alas, this new kind of thought kept on returning, I'm Not OK was getting established.

So I went to call on Mike in his little house and said my say: "I came to tell you I'm sorry I talked about you behind your back." He stuck out his hand: "That took real guts. Thanks!"

Since that day I haven't seen anything more of Mike. But I know he and I retain a warm spot in our hearts for each other.

A Measure

In order to insure that it was God's voice and not my own, I was encouraged to measure these written-down thoughts by the four standards and then share them with friends equally dedicated to doing His will. Evidently it was possible to confuse the two sources, God's and mine, and since now the Compliant part of my Adaptive Child was regnant, this seemed eminently reasonable. It helped to forge links between all of us and to formalize our need for each other.

I took to writing the standards down first thing and then seeing what ideas came under each heading. Obviously I had fallen down in many ways over the years. The Lord would say what, if anything, needed to be done about each thing.

Under "absolute honesty" soon came memories of those earliest lies of childhood that I had told my father when sitting on the toilet and pretending that I had "gone" when I hadn't. I was beginning to welcome openness and hate the shame that concealed. Since he was living in Washington and I was in Miami, I wrote a full account of these happenings and apologized for the resentments I had felt against him.

He replied that he guessed he had not been as good a father as he thought he was. He was sorry for that.

Later I learned from Charles that Father had been completely nonplussed by these confessions and had consulted Charles as a doctor as to what they could all mean. Charles had told him that it was probably homosexuality coming out. I wasn't too grateful to Charles for this supposed elucidation for which he apologizes himself.

I found in my study of MRA material that it doesn't matter that all the steps taken in restitution or under guidance don't have happy results. What counts is obedience and the change that the Almighty is bringing in ourselves through carrying them out. Frank Buchman, MRA's founder, had talked of "driving in stakes." The discomfort of an apology, the blow to one's pride, would effectively prevent repetition of the offenses in question. God respected the other person's free will in deciding on a response—not all could be favorable.

The Feeling of Guidance

Before going on to tell more of the happenings of that eventful first spring with MRA, may I elaborate a little on "guidance" itself.

I kept on with the practice of writing down those four standards and then seeing what thoughts came in relation to each one, for many months. Gradually a feel was built up that such and such was truly guidance, a clear pipeline was constructed and I decided that I no longer needed that as a starter—or crutch—the feel was unmistakably there. The voice was virtually audible. I may say it still is.

Elements in this often coming at the beginning of the time were comforting and repetitive, thus indicating that Nurturing Parent was involved. When later I was to have guidance with Russell and Lucy, they would laugh with me because they knew the first thought I inevitably wrote down was: "All is well!" Although all in the world is dramatically not well, this reflected and reflects as I write it down still, an inner health and rightness in my basic position, an I'm OK—You're OK of the soul.

There often followed a sense of oneness with the universe and a realization of the love for me of a supreme being, before more individuated thoughts came about others or things to be done.

The result is a joy that keeps night problems and anxieties—Spooky's offspring—from entering the day or weighing down a week or a month. It's like scrubbing the blackboard clean each morning.

Most recently, when fearfully certain strains came into my relations with the group and I had to proceed on my own, there kept coming, as it had for so many years, the clear words: "No fear!" This I can translate more fully as meaning: Don't let Spooky down you; trust your Free Child, your Little Professor! But I'm anticipating the newness that you'll find in the third part of this book.

For nothing in this world would I go back on my decision made so many years ago to have a time of quiet in the early morning and write the thoughts down!

Belief in God

You, gentle reader, may be surprised to find me at a certain point expressing a belief in God when earlier I had certainly run therefrom.

I believe it's a mistake to think of a belief in God in the abstract as that we have it or we don't. I feel it is so closely connected with our life position that it most readily flows from or comes along with that.

As long as I was basically in Vengeful Child—I'm OK—*They* are not OK—reflecting the resentments against the parent figures of childhood, it would be virtually impossible to believe in a spiritual divine parent behind and above the hated tyrant figures. Lucifer was the mythical hero both in the *Paradise Lost* I pored over and as I've said in *Revolte des Anges.*

Once my basic life position changed into I'm Not OK—*They* are OK, "*They*" could be not only my new friends and the newly accepted leaders, but I could visualize a new friend in heaven. Jesus began to emerge from the subconscious where He had always had a place. God was no longer an Old Testament tyrant whose freaky behavior I could spell out only too skillfully, but a Nurturing and Loving Father, as we shall see in the section on "Presumption."

Interestingly enough, along with this came for the first time an acceptance that perhaps the afterlife the religions talked about might be possible. On one especial night and morning that first spring, I had a sense of *presence.* Coupled with a decision to give up the last tie to tobacco—I had reduced it to three corncobs a day—was a strong certainty that there did exist a thereafter in which I could take part. Whereas before I would have rejected this scornfully in my best twentieth-century scepticism, I now felt it boldly enough to tell George Fraser and the other friends about it. They stroked me therefor.

Now that I'm moving, as you will find in Part Three of this account, towards a third life position: I'm OK—You/They are OK, I don't feel all the certainty I did. But I do find a peaceful acceptance. And along with that a faith that key thoughts can come in my quiet times and that there is protection, healing and love hovering constantly over me.

Dellwood and Frank Buchman

I had been not only attending "team" meetings of the travelling "full-time" group but much larger gatherings, which were often scheduled in the county auditorium, at which various leaders spoke. As I sat in the rear and looked at those seated on the platform, I singled out in my mind a dynamic dark-haired Englishman of about my own age. This was Peter Howard, a well-known journalist who had startled the London literary world by giving up a brilliant career to pursue MRA, and whose books I was to delight in one after another.

Afterwards, in trying to explain what happened next, I was driven to the concept of devil possession. Put it now if you wish that my Vengeful Child still had a great grip and that in my lust to put somebody of power and position down in this group that struck me as faultless, almost inevitably I picked the most intellectual.

I was burning. The struggle was between two ego states in Child—Rebellious and Compliant.

Frank Buchman, founder of the movement, was at Dellwood, large country estate in Mount Kisco, New York, given to MRA by Emily Hammond. He was thus following a practice that was often his of leaving direct responsibility in the hands of others, even though the Miami campaign was so crucial to his plans of massive intervention in the airline industry.

One morning I conceived the idea that I should go see him and tell him his movement was in bad hands, that changes should be made. I got hold of Bruce, who had often given my thoughts a complaisant approval, and told him I was "guided" to go see Frank Buchman.

He telephoned the illustrious sage, got a cheerful invitation, and before hours had passed, we were together on a plane bound for New York. With the shrewdness of a child who wants his own way, I had neglected to consult with others of our friends who, I suspected, might not have acceded to the plan quite so readily.

This was the first of many hundreds of dashes by air that Moral Re-Armament was to bring my way.

We were ushered into a large, cool house. Frank Buchman

would see me the next morning, Sunday, at ten o'clock. There was a little elegant study, all leather, bound books and hunting prints where just the two of us met. He had some difficulty; in the quiet I could hear his breath come and go as he listened with gracious awareness.

I told him that Peter Howard was an ambitious man and therefore couldn't be "God-controlled." He asked what indications I had of this, and gave an anecdote of his own trust in his friend. I went on—eventually bringing forth the core thought that it was I who should lead the legions and be the mouthpiece for the Almighty's commands.

He, who had been so self-effacingly giving me all his attention, encouraging with these positive strokes of care, said sharply: "No!"

He asked of my family, Norris left on the Keys, whom I wanted to see. He said: "Stay around a while. Don't go back. There will be time to talk. Don't be in a hurry. I must go to church now in the village. Peter Howard [sic!] is giving the sermon. We will see you at lunch."

Flight

The house was empty. I went upstairs, put my things in a bag, left a note on the dresser and crept out the big front door, convinced "they" would be after me soon. I walked down the country road, suitcase in hand, not knowing which direction was which. Though not used to hitchhiking, I put out a thumb when a little truck came along and soon I was headed into town! The man smiled.

Once safe in the big city, I sent off a telegram to Norris, saying I had quit Moral Re-Armament, thus pacifying her growing objections to a movement that seemed to expect total involvement.

The next day, in connection with a hurried train trip to New Haven to collect some cash, I was completely alone, dwarfed in the great hall of Grand Central Station with thousands hurrying as always to and fro under the vaulted ceiling. As I looked at them, I had the clear overpowering feeling: "You are the worst one of all. There is not one that is as bad as you."

This marked the final passing of control from Vengeful Child to Compliant (Guilty) Child. I haven't looked back since that day—though often angered momentarily with vengeful reaction.

I sent off another telegram to Norris, this time saying I was returning to Florida and rejoining Moral Re-Armament. Whether, isolated on the coral island, she ever received these contradictory reports or what she thought of them, I do not know.

One objection that had jumped briefly into my consciousness over Dr. Buchman's invitation to stay on at Dellwood was that it was immoral and uncaring for me thus to leave my wife alone in the Keys. Later, after I had returned and unsuccessfully bombarded her with many words in favor of MRA and attempted changes, I was to think: "Frank knew I had to change first. If only I had listened to him!"

Soon the giant Constellation was winging me back to Miami.

You will remember how ambition to be biggest and best had kept me going on the farm.

This characteristic, the thrust for success, did certainly not die the instant I crossed the threshold into a moral religious movement. It was the mechanism known as *projection* by which we throw the image of our own problems onto the faces of others, that had led me thus to pick out Peter Howard and say what I had to Frank Buchman. Both of these men were to play significant parts in my life, which this incident only foreshadowed.

However, for now I couldn't face Frank for any length of time such as he had suggested—I was too Not-OK. It was necessary to get back to the pleasant involvement that had opened up in Miami and the friends already made.

Presumption

George Fraser and I had long discussions on what I had felt that had led to this flight. Very humbly his guidance was that he wasn't competent to deal with all these matters, but what he did see was presumption in me. A baby, newly arrived in a family, doesn't immediately take over and start telling the parents and the rest of the family what to do. I was still a babe.

Mackinac Island in the Great Lakes had some years since been chosen as summer gathering place for the MRA conferences in the U.S. This year was to bring all the fruit of the Miami work, mechanics, foremen, labor leaders, pilots, management to add color to the international team. In preparation for this, one day a train, laden with full-time workers, departed from the Miami station for the north. The take-off was delayed as hundreds said fond farewells to their new friends on platforms and train-coach steps.

I was suddenly alone in a vast city where so much had been going on. There was no invitation for me to Mackinac. Perhaps rumors of my runoff to New York had reached the ears of those responsible. It would take time to win any confidence from them.

In a bathing suit I went over to the Crandon Park beach. There, in the brilliant sun or under the same trees where earlier I had worked on a novel, over long days I tried to think out this matter of presumption. Accepting it as true, why would I especially be prey to such an offense?

Strangely, as I considered, surrounded by the crowds of bathers and the warm seas, something close to what TA would give came as explanation. I was presumptuous because I did not really believe in the love of the Father God. I had to force myself on His attention!

Now that I thought about it, I did believe in His love and goodness. It would not be necessary to presume again.

Several letters of apology went off to Frank. But I wasn't to hear from him for some time.

I will draw a quick veil over the summer and the unsuccessful efforts to win Norris to this new philosophy. The time was spent between Dellwood and Salem, where our little family was to spend their last summer. I cannot remember whether it was that October or a year later that I made the first trip to Mackinac

Island. Gradually I was learning the ways of the new life and the unsympathetic reactions it produced in others.

Divorce

In my first flush of enthusiasm I had assumed, of course, everybody would welcome the new truths and jump for joy to be shown the way. Surprisingly enough, not all did. In fact, that first spring when I had written some of my brothers about it, they had indicated they didn't even want to see me! This was flabbergasting.

One of the cardinal demonstrations in which MRA had improved homelife was increased participation by the husbands in household duties. In line with this I had taken delight both in washing the dishes and doing any other chores within my capacity. Norris wasn't impressed: "Big deal—a few dishes!"

She still felt I was talking too much about it. Around the area she found sympathetic counselors who told her it was insupportable.

One crowning blow was evidently a talk with Bruce when he told her proudly that the initiates, the most committed to MRA, no longer had sexual relations between husband and wife, except when they were "guided" to have children. This was unheard of!

She took steps for divorce and we worked out a separation agreement.

I was distressed and felt lost, though I knew her affection had cooled some years before. I was turning to God for direction; couldn't He help in this situation?

She may have been touched by my sincere pleas. She came up with a proposition: for the sake of the children and the continuation of a home for them, she would give up this other man if I in return would give up Moral Re-Armament. We could go on together.

I, who had escaped from the void on the Keys, who had found a faith and a usefulness, who believed for the first time in a Deity beyond my own nose, who was now a part of a world "organism," could not accept this. True, that to belong I was following a path of I'm Not OK—only They (the leaders) are OK, but I was reaping the rewarding corollary which any organization gives: *We are OK—You (the outside world) are Not OK*—because you need to change. It would be unthinkable to betray the new-found cause.

In quiet I thought of a compromise. I would no longer work with my new friends; I would find some other job. But I would still rise early and write down my thoughts in the "little black book" in which I had formed the habit of jotting down "guidance." God could still direct—it was His suggestion.

But she would have none of it. The divorce moved on its inexorable way and was completed in 1952.

The Children—Nat

Although the separation and divorce was to be a trauma for the children, I haven't wanted to give before and after pictures of them which wouldn't fit the flow of my own memories, although theirs may be sharply distinct.

Within a month of the final decree, Norris was married again and settled with her husband, Wesley Fowler, in a trailer south of Miami from which later she was to move further south but still within easy reach. Russell and Lucy were able to visit me each weekend, so that there was a continuity of seeing them which the divorce only formalized.

The news of our breaking up had hit Nat hard the summer before. Thirteen at that time, I remember his lying on the bed in his room face down. I was surprised that he felt it so much and felt clumsily unable to give much comfort. His usual Be-Strong impassivity and acceptance of most everything, temporarily laid aside, had caught me without enough openness of heart to tell him all I had been feeling. It would be many years before I would know enough to do that.

Faithfully in accordance with the precept Be Honest, and dogmatically because there were many current MRA stories of parents creating new relationships with their children by telling all, I was to reveal to him in the next years my sexual misadventures and some of the color of my past. He heard me out politely and I fantasized great results. The intimacy I sought has come more recently in simpler, less ritualistic ways of candor about all feelings, not just sex.

No matter how well hidden—My Way is Better than Yours, or My Group is Better Than Yours vitiate the great love which can come when parents and children live I'm OK—You're OK.

The Children—Russell

Nat, though tall, is lanky like his father. Toughened by the outdoor life, his body responds well to the demands he's made on it. Russell, on the other hand, was a stocky, strong bundle of energy as a boy, who was to grow into a robust, genial, attractive man, equally tall.

You recall how by the time Russell was born, I had decided that my heart needed to be given to each child. Russell and I have always been close friends. This is one of the joys of life.

However, in those last bad days before the divorce, I used to get irritated. Critical Parent was waiting to take command once more. I would get angry at Russell, then seven.

On one occasion especially, in the trailer which I hadn't yet left, I struck him in anger over some trivial offense.

This wasn't love. I knew it was wrong. Soon I apologized. This he accepted with all the grace with which children forgive an erring but repentant parent.

I went outside and walked up and down in the dusk. I had read in the MRA literature that sin must be hated. This I did hate and hated myself. Never again was I to strike anyone. Guidance called for honesty with my teammates the next day. "Poor little fellow," one of them said. And I told my mother about it which I didn't want to do.

Thus, character was changing and Critical Parent left behind at least as far as action is concerned.

I haven't any account from Russell of how the split affected him. He seems to have emerged relatively unscathed from the wounds of those years.

The Children—Lucy

Almost from birth Lucy had been a baby whose eyes, though dark, were bright and took in everything. One of my best drawings was made of her in the crib, alert, alive. She was sensitive and childhood was not to be easy for her.

We have grown to be loving friends and she has told me a lot of all she went through. It's not easy to remember that for long there was much she couldn't say, walled in as children are by the very force of their feelings.

She was petite and, aside from the early asthma, never ate very heartily. She insisted on few items only, mainly vegetables—"rabbit food" we used to call it. We were concerned but found that some people just do grow more slowly. Later she would eat anything and grow to a respectable height.

There were bouts in hospital and attacks of pneumonia. She tells of early fear of being left alone in the hospital and ascribes the asthma to coming on after this fear.

Pearl Daniels, the loyal servant I mentioned earlier, gave her heart to Lucy with unstinting love which helped bring her through.

Down on the Keys her dancing eyes won a natural favor and Russell uncomfortably thought a few times it might have been better if he'd been a girl. But she became a loyal sister and followed his lead for many years doing all the bold things he did. Through the difficult years they clung to each other.

The breach was a blow. She couldn't understand why "Daddy" was leaving and felt cruelly that I no longer loved her. Told that God was taking me away, she hated God. This has persisted as embedded in Child. And though Adult may have other thoughts, she may not want to consider a supreme being at all.

Guidance at Brickell Avenue

When Russell and Lucy visited me over the weekends at Brickell Avenue, I used to take them to the major park playgrounds in Miami. A favorite occupation was also Putt-Putt, and we became quite expert at sinking the long caroms.

One day at play I had tried to do all the things they did. This lasted less than half an hour at the end of which, exhausted, I realized I could enjoy my children endlessly but never keep up.

They, too, had "little black books" in which they would put down their thoughts. Before Lucy could write, I would write them down at her dictation. These thoughts were simple and good; they enjoyed doing it as part of fellowship with Daddy. Whether or not she objected, Lucy went along on the surface.

When Wes and Norris decided to move further away and settle in the Bahamas, we had a farewell day and party. The children brought me the books a little sadly and said: "You keep them for us." I had toyed with an unrealistic hope that they could go on with it on their own. It was associated with me and they knew that without the motivation it couldn't be kept up.

I watched them go off kicking their heels on the pilot house of the rented boat and then came back to the house in tears. For long I cherished the photos we had taken on that occasion, showing us united, blowing out the candles on a cake especially baked.

Lifechanging

In my usual fashion, I had been reading all the available MRA literature from the earliest theologically-weighted books of the Oxford Group to Peter Howard's sparkling analyses putting the movement into a world setting, and Frank Buchman's own limpid but electric addresses. Here I found a term for helping people called "*lifechanging*"—evidently the ultimately satisfying occupation of the "changed" person when he has changed enough to be able to "meet the needs" of others. There were lively stories of Frank Buchman himself doing this as he had since the day of his own first change.

To be a "lifechanger" was to have arrived in Moral Re-Armament. I longed for this ability which would mean acquiring some of that potency which had eluded me since in childhood I had dreamed of the Wishing Ring.

With Bruce McCay, a young Miamian, ex-soldier, who had decided to throw in his lot full-time a few years before, I began to visit some of the homes of those workers in the airlines who had expressed an interest. These were young mechanics in Eastern Airlines, one of the major beneficiaries of the campaign. Thus began a fascinating and rewarding effort which was to take me into homes in many parts of the world and net me many hundreds of friends, whom to this day I think of with gratitude. They have been so gracious!

Gradually as we went along, it dawned on me that those we were seeing would not necessarily go through the miraculous stages described in Frank Buchman's initiatives. That might be happening elsewhere—it might result in the stories I heard from the public platforms, it would remain for me as a shimmering pot of gold which the rainbow would ever promise.

Thus developed two aspects of the life I was living. One, the joy of friendship which, as I said, has been solid. The other the realization that "pushing" was wrong and I must be content with the effort and not the result. As experience widened and I "followed through" with more and more of those whom the work has touched, it became more and more clear that the undertaking was the worthwhile thing and not what might or might not happen to those whom one was seeing.

Compassion more recently has shown me that change is such a delicate flower that laying any hands of my own on it is enough to prevent its further growth, or claiming it in any way as my work is enough to turn it off forever.

But in those days I had to swallow disappointment. For example, one young couple were Jewish. The wife became a lively outgoing friend, as well as the husband. However, in reading Buchman's speeches she came across references to the "Cross of Christ" and cooled in going further into something which threatened her ties to the religion of her fathers. I knew nothing of and cared little for the symbols of organized religion, but failed to persuade her that the emphasis was really on behavior. We remained the best of friends.

Talking Too Much

Seeing people obviously involves talking. There was much to talk about and to learn on both sides. I was always fascinated with the human side of the operation of an airline—these men and their jobs and the complex relationships with each other. We were expected to give some ideas about Moral Re-Armament in general and how it had worked out in other times and places. Bruce even while in the service had helped to start it again in Italy in the later war years.

He talked a lot. My problem of silence exploded in expressions of resentment a few times—cashing in brown stamps as TA would say—without bringing on noticeable change in him.

We meet many people who talk a lot or too much. In their book, "Remaking Men," which was one of the ones I most esteemed, Peter Howard and Paul Campbell, physician to Frank Buchman, have this to say:

> The secret of changing people is to listen. We are most talkative when we have least peace of heart. We hold the conversation when we are least centered in others and most centered in ourselves. It is a way we have for getting into the picture and staying there . . . When we talk too much it is in the erroneous belief that what we say is more important than what anyone else has to say . . .

I loved this passage and would quote it whenever I could, feeling superior because *I* didn't talk so much—whereas thanks were really due to my script and not to my virtue!

What I would add now would be an appraisal of those who do have this failing. As so often when in Parent, as that book so often is, we blame the person or at least the action as a whole—

"self-centered," etc. As though the talker did this deliberately.

I sense an insecurity—a Not-OKness, the fundamental one Thomas Harris postulates, which the talker covers up with many spoken words. Even more I feel there is a dissatisfied heart, probably stroke-hungry, as Steiner suggests. This makes the person redouble the effort to gain the strokes he or she cannot admit to wanting—the Be-Strong driver keeps us from that.

Banging negatively at such a person is not likely to help them; surprising them with positive strokes might. To do this requires the insight of Little Professor, not the blows of Vengeful Child who'd like to do a little talking himself, as I did. We can never answer a problem which we have potentially ourselves. Talking too little is the reverse of the same coin as talking too much.

Sex a No-No!

In the meantime with brother Bruce and others I was learning what it means to live by those four standards.

Sex, as I suggested earlier, had been announced as incompatible with "absolute purity." Thus, most firmly in this respect as well as in many others, the requirements were for obedience to the earliest no-nos contained in Parent. Sexual pleasure is out; don't feel; consider your feelings to be temptations to sin. God can give you power enough to conquer what in your own strength you can't deal with.

As I would go downtown on the errands which my job as helper-of-all-trades required, my eyes would pick out attractive pairs of feminine legs—in those days skirts in Miami were ultra short! Some days were worse than others. It was painful but I felt "victory," i.e., freedom from such excess concern, was certain. And eventually it did fade and I could take some comfort in a new-found "liberty."

It is true that my main concern was and has remained people and what goes on inside them—not flesh for its own sake.

Here is a footnote to the campaign of MRA in the airlines.

One or two couples decided to have no more sex and went around enjoining this decision on their friends with the fervor that often springs from: "If we decide so and so, so can you!"

The enthusiasm with which the work in Miami had flowered—the real progress in human relations—began to wither under this forced restriction, too arduous for the free-and-easy airline folk. Once backing away, they remained outwardly friendly but inwardly cool. From then on we would be battling ghosts and shadows.

Mackinac Island

The years after meeting MRA were mostly spent at our family home at 2025 Brickell Avenue in Miami, which had gradually become a center for that work, with up to fifteen people staying there at a time. Mother generously gave the use of it for that purpose.

However, the effort in the summers was towards a much larger center abuilding on Mackinac Island, Michigan, and I took to going there to help with the operation and as a place at which my children could visit and gain what I hoped they would in this setting with many young and old.

How to describe in a few words this northern jewel set among pines and the deep blue of freezing Lake Huron? It commanded the enthusiasm of many from all across Canada and the U.S., as well as other nations. Every phase of operation and expansion was underlined with dedicatory hope. Movies were made, songs written, campaigns assisted from such far lands as Japan, Taiwan, the Philippines, Brazil, to mention only a few.

Fortunately this is not a history of MRA of which there are many, but of my personal adventures as I came athwart this colorful movement among the episodes of a life; I need not tell all the hows and whys of its workings. Basically being there was not easy personally. I had to stretch. The new basic life position I'd taken, I'm Not OK—They're OK, was often called upon to help undergo these difficulties. Since that was the position and I enjoyed negative strokes therefrom as well as the positive of which there were still plenty, it was all right and acceptable.

Some sharp vignettes follow of MRA life as I experienced it in those years, the intensity of which make them stand out.

The first summer at Dellwood, I was following in tandem a supposedly "guided" teammate on a trip to Idlewild Airport to pick up arrivals—I didn't know the way myself. He drove like a fiend, way over any speed limit. I gulped, bethought me of the Almighty, did the best I could to keep him in sight, and somehow arrived. It was puzzling.

One summer at Mackinac. A lovely cottage where Dr. Buchman was staying himself and many rich meals were served on beautiful china which had been donated, with up to thirty at a time. Day after day I washed those dishes by hand—they were too nice for any machine. He never spoke to me about it; I was not invited to one of those meals myself; I felt that was an OK treatment for the presumption I had shown.

But washing all those elegant dishes, as I had also done at Dellwood, I came to love fine china. With my aesthetic sense I guess I would have had to learn to wash them with appreciation or not at all. Duty alone wouldn't have done it; there would have been breakage.

At the end of the season I paid for an elevator for the cottage. He had had to be carried up narrow stairs all season, as at that time he couldn't walk—I had watched this many times.

Thus, gracefully and with a master hand did Frank help a person like me to live in the I'm Not OK—You're OK quadrant!

Another summer at the reception desk of a new residence building. The job was much like a hotel clerk's as there were constant comings and goings. The phone kept ringing—I made notes.

It was impossible to deal with every request, which would have required three phones and several people to go here or there. So I committed the business to God—after all, it was His—wrote the things down, floated "through the feathers" and found that miraculously things often settled themselves and came to the surface, when for a while the water had seemed too deep.

One of the high points and also most difficult was a month in the kitchen, where male help had been requested, and seven hundred people were being cared for. My awkwardness was in evidence, and at the end of that time it was gently suggested I serve elsewhere. I had learned a lot.

The Children at Mackinac

Not all that I had hoped would happen to the children came to them on their visits to Mackinac. Since my Adaptive Child was in command in those years, conforming came natural to me. For them other facets of Child were predominant and thus made it less so.

Nat came a couple of times. The young people who devoted themselves to him had perhaps rather heavy-handed methods of "sharing" their own "sins" on purity and then expecting reciprocation. He soon told me he was fond of me personally but had had enough of it and was leaving.

I arranged to meet him with some of his belongings on the dock to say farewell. Every move on or off the island had to be timed to the boat schedule.

Somehow I arrived with one of his suitcases at the wrong dock—there were several competing boat lines. I could hear him shouting across the water as departure time approached.

This error—evidently my Parent disapproval of his plan was sufficient to warp my love—adds one more to the list of bitter memories which my relationship with him evoke. I shipped him the bag. And, as I can never tire of saying, his forgiveness has been magnanimous.

Russell, being six years younger and remarkably flexible, got by more easily. Or he has never wanted to complain if things were hard. Two memories stand out.

There was bad blood between some of the village folk who

supposedly were either in the pay of the "interests" or morally "defeated," and ourselves. Children reflect the prejudices of their parents. A small gang invaded our end of the town and threw pebbles at some of the MRA children. Russell defended Lucy and the others with vigor.

He was a helper one summer in the supply room right under the kitchen where I worked. Hand trolleys laden with milk and other provisions were brought up by freight elevator from below. He would push one of these trolleys with such enthusiasm down the kitchen aisles that the lady cooks would have to skip nimbly aside!

His boss there that season was a rough-and-ready young man named Charley Brown, skilled mechanic and capable organizer. Occasionally he would bethink himself of his obligation to do something morally for Russell. Russ, as I call him, would see him coming, much as I used to see my athletic mentor in my days at school, and hide quickly in the big walk-in coolers. This experience didn't seem to harm either his body or his good temper.

Lucy's stays were less obviously one thing or another. Our love has usually reached out to bridge unsaid things.

The children preferred to eat in the cafeteria, which took care of kitchen and dining room volunteers, the paid help and excess personnel, who liked the informality of trays better than family-style service.

But many days at lunch Lucy would eat nothing and remain silent. Holding her hand, completely baffled, I would walk her back to the gingerbread-style wooden house where we slept. After some hours she would come with a throbbing voice: "I'm sorry, Daddy!"

It was not till many many years later that she explained to what this was due. Late morning was the hour when the mail-room doors were thrown open and we would line up for our letters. Often there was no letter for Lucy from her mother, whom she missed a lot. She couldn't express this disappointment in words, it was too deep—but expressed it instead in the withdrawal.

I am sometimes sensitive, but this I never guessed.

CHAPTER EIGHT

Out to the World

"If you are changed, you naturally want to change other people. The next thing is you want to save civilization. Then you want to reach the millions out there. It is a natural programme."

That is a quotation from Frank Buchman's perhaps most challenging speech, "Revival, Revolution, Renaissance," made at Visby in Sweden in 1938.

Once accepted as a loyal "changed" follower and member of the "force," it was natural for me, too, to consider taking the message out to the world. During the next fifteen years, with some interruption, that was the background I operated in.

The same influences that had brought an international group to Miami, that had built up the center on Mackinac Island, were moving around the other nations and continents.

Europe "On the Road"

A newly-written musical called "The Vanishing Island," by Peter Howard, with which travelled men of leadership attainment, had achieved amazing successes in East Asia, bringing reconciliation to some of the bitter adversaries of the War in the Pacific. After coming back to the West through the Middle East and reaching Caux, it was preparing for a European tour.

I was set to join it there and arrived with my mother and Henry in Germany on the way. There she fell ill and had to have a serious operation, so I stayed on in Munich with them till she recovered enough to return to the U.S.

Thus I never got to Caux that year (1955) but had an extraordinary experience "on the road" in Switzerland, Finland, Sweden, Norway, Denmark, Switzerland again for Christmas and on to Milan and the workers' suburb of Sesto San Giovanni, and Paris in the Théâtre des Champs Elysées, where I had enjoyed concerts as a student. Everywhere we went we were met by overflow crowds and theaters so packed I could rarely get in to see the show myself. Night after night we saw "the millions" at our door.

Two aspects of this experience stand out in memory. One, I had trouble fitting in as a helper, unlike most of the previous years. Two American men were running the "book" team—much literature was sold every evening and the supplies had to be procured, maintained and selling arranged for. Younger "full-time" people were being trained in each country to handle this kind of responsibility.

I enjoyed these younger associates; I enjoyed selling in the aisles or at book tables, or handling piles and piles of books and pictorials. One of these bosses puzzled me, however, with the rarity of good strokes he gave out and the vindictiveness of negative strokes with which he rewarded my labors. Evidently I lacked the initiative he expected and my passivity in waiting for instructions hooked his Critical Parent all too often.

As my basic position in those years was I'm Not OK—They (the leaders) are OK, I was sure somehow he was right without knowing what I could do about it. *Compliant Child is not Creative Child, though many efforts have been made to force this coalition.*

But these two were only sergeants or lieutenants in the hierarchy of the team.

At the huge team meetings we had every day—there were several hundred of us on the tour—I could relish an obscure seat among the crowd and drink in the wisdom of the august. The author of the play, Peter Howard, had perhaps most to say and to give. His thought sparkled without restraint. I had long since shifted from criticism to admiration of this colorful chief.

Though he would often publicly chastise some erring subaltern, these were usually among the experienced men. I was too invisible and in truth too meek to have provoked his censure.

After my return to America I wrote him about that return and was delighted to get a caring, humorous reply. From then on we corresponded and though I was usually uncomfortable with him face to face, a pen friendship grew up which was to give me rich strokes thenceforth.

Father's Death

Early in the new year I was suddenly summoned home. Father was dying.

His last years had been somewhat restricted by heart weakness. In those years all of us brothers had gathered with him a few times when he had received us graciously and smiled with leonine acceptance: "These are my cubs." I had been to see him alone on the top floor of the house on F Street where Suzanne, our stepmother, watched every move and kept my visit to half an hour. We had fenced some on the moral aspects of life. He smiled at some of my questions but said little.

This time it was too late for any more exchange. I and Bruce, the brother who has so often appeared when I am most in need, stayed in the luxurious MRA home of the Elys on Massachusetts Avenue. We crept into the hospital, where Father was in a final coma and prayed together in his room in a way that persuaded us he could hear even if he couldn't respond.

In a few more days came the funeral at Arlington, with the formality and the salutes.

Consciously I took refuge in faith and was happy that we had seemingly conveyed our love.

Underneath was preparing a considerable collapse. I had been months in Europe on a very irregular and unbalanced diet, and often with no more than three or four hours sleep a night—even for me who am trained for little, that is not enough.

There was an errand to be done for my co-workers involving a message to some dignitary in the Pentagon. That is a large and confusing place to find one's way around in. I wandered and was finally met by a handsome, bemedalled officer who escorted me out with great grace.

But the building remained in its squat, fort-like menace as a nightmare apparition. I found myself in bed with the doctor called. He said there was nothing wrong with me that rest and vitamins couldn't cure.

We were shipped off to Miami, me to rest and Bruce as good samaritan and shepherd.

Recovery

It's as though the spring of the watch was broken. For weeks I did nothing—I suppose I took care of the body's needs. But I sat outdoors on the lawn of that lovely property, absorbed the health-giving light and air, and let time pass. This was of all the times in my life perhaps the one when I was longest in the despair position: I'm Not OK—Nothing's OK.

Thoughts were not circulating. Eventually, with images of Mother in mind, faint echoes of incest, I climbed out. I was to resume the normal day-to-day activity of an MRA worker whose property was at the disposal of his organization.

However, in considering this strange period since then, I recognize two possible gambits of Child thought.

One the loss of Father, the model of Nurturing Parent on whom I was building so much, may have been an undercutting blow to the worthwhileness of such imitation. "What's it all for it it winds us up like that?" Child may have been asking.

The other is along the same line. I had been living within Compliant Child's direction. To the commands: "You will *never* attain. Do as I (Parent) say," I had been replying, "OK, I will!" Most of the MRA stories had fairy tale endings: "And so they lived happily ever after." Yet Father hadn't accepted much from me after his initial apology, and now he was gone in a very final way.

I clung to the security of my idea: I'm Not OK—You (the leaders) are OK, so that when I felt stronger it was intact. These questions never surfaced into consciousness at that time. My Be Strong driver, Don't Feel injunction, would keep them hidden and disallow grief, even the natural grief over a loved one's death.

Eric Berne says that after the living parent's death, the script Parent often fastens on us more securely than ever. Evidently this doesn't happen without some stress.

Frank in My Home

Toward the end of the next summer at Mackinac, I had once again invited Frank Buchman to visit our home in Miami, stooping towards him as he sat in his wheel chair outdoors one warm afternoon. I was pleasantly surprised to have him accept: "I'll come to that Binkel place of yours."

That slip of the tongue—we called it "Brickell" after the well-known avenue which ran along the front—is typical of Frank and illustrates the quasi-humorous way in which he allowed himself to make mistakes. In contrast to most of us in MRA who have been rigorously driven by a Be Perfect driver, and in remarkable contrast to his own teaching in perfection of detail, he allowed himself errors and lapses of memory without loss of aplomb. His secretary, Morris Martin, a scholar who was to appear in Miami with him, often was expected miraculously to supply names or fill in with stories when Frank had merely indicated: " . . . You know, that feller . . . !"

Brewster and Frances, his wife, were already at Brickell. We prepared somewhat feverishly for Frank's coming. It was decided that my house, the elegant building on the avenue which I had purchased as a former part of the estate a couple of years before, should house him and those of his staff that could fit into it.

Slowly we began to install an elevator—this inconveniently wasn't finished for some time after his arrival.

It was implied I hadn't been tough enough with contractors to push it through when needed. Here, as often in my life, my Please Me (please them) driver finds discomfort in not pleasing all parties at once and not being hardboiled when needed.

Frank was not to be at all well that winter and spent much time in his room. It was thought to be his heart but many tests showed that his lungs also needed attention. By the next year he had moved to a drier climate.

A Christmas Party

This meant that the times we spent with him became noteworthy. Of these the Christmas party was the most dramatic.

I had heard of Christmases with "Poppa" Frank as being inspiring with their tender sentiment and good cheer. This was not to be the atmosphere of that memorable occasion.

Frank had been expected to stay in bed. We were having tea when it was announced he was coming down.

If ever there was a man in Critical Parent, he was it that day. Only one escaped the lash as he singled us out one after another for attention to the specific things we had been or were doing. The one was Rachel Jackson, the marvelous, dignified black lady from Washington who had been doing some of his cooking.

She was the kind who always called me "Mr. Bingham," no matter how free we became with each other.

He sat her next to him in the tall-windowed living room and after each sally would lean towards her and screw up his face in a colossal wink! This shows in a capsule how his battle for real I'm OK—You're OK between the races never left him and how he was combining Spunky fun with the Parent help to each of us.

I didn't escape. As the host I was expected to play Santa Claus. The barrage had left me tongue-tied; my Please-Me driver, which was usually hooked by Frank, paralyzed me with fright as to what was coming next. Was there no pleasing him? The very lesson he was trying to teach us was: "Please God, don't consider any human, even me."

He turned his eyes upward to where I was standing: "If you were like this at a party, they'd all leave!" How true—*Living Statue* is not the merriest of hosts! I blundered ahead with my duties distributing the presents.

Towards the end he was helped to his feet. And as we surrounded him, he changed. I didn't know how to put it into words then, but from Critical Parent he switched to Compliant Child, the ego state we were in most of the time.

Reverently he said: "We are mean and despicable. But we can be glad and grateful."

Then he left us.

In my quiet time the next morning I thought of how he had given each of us what we needed. We often told that story on ourselves.

Now I would add that like most figures who live in Parent much of the time, he didn't distinguish between Nurturing Parent and Critical Parent. He well knew the nurturing care for the disturbed soul. It never occurred to him that the Critical Parent rebuke which elicited apology and change from the faithful around him drew it from Compliant Child as it did me without freeing the person to seek the Almighty and find in Him a fresh breeze, a "self-rolling wheel," without in a word freeing Free Child or the creative Little Professor.

I gather, too, in considering this story and others about him that he managed to include his own Free Child, to let it out and have fun. In that way he was a more complete man and more effective than those who remain uniquely in Parent or Adult. I have a hunch it hurt him when we stayed in fearful Spooky and tried to please him so much of the time; this would help to explain the critical outbursts.

He quite often surprised me by preferring the company of simple people—I believe these were those in whom Compliant Child was less developed and with whom he could exchange Free-Child Child strokes.

Within these contradictions, implicit perhaps in all leadership, were to grow the discordant elements which later were to burst the structure so confidently and gloriously built during his creative life. I am encouraged to think that leaders with a knowledge of TA and their own different ego states can in the future avoid these pitfalls. But I am anticipating with generalities.

Caux and South America

A few years later saw me at Caux in Switzerland. It was to be the last summer of Frank's life.

In this account of my life adventures I haven't put much stress on the strife of others except where it affected me deeply. For instance, I gave no account of my parents' divorce in my young manhood—it didn't strike me profoundly.

At Caux that summer we Americans were put under a lot of pressure to change; Peter Howard led us day after day in what he called a conference within a conference. But I wasn't involved very personally.

I had been thrilled that Frank had had guidance one morning to invite Bruce, Frances and myself to Caux. In less than twenty-four hours we were on the transatlantic flight, I from Miami, they from Mackinac.

It flattered my esteem to be included in this struggle of the heavies. I had never taken it on myself to lead—I could hardly be blamed for having led wrongly.

I was to learn through these years to try to deal with what I could see. But Compliant Child's attitude is so They are OK that I could hardly not take for granted the certainties of those who boldly seemed to know. I watched. Questions were not to come for some years yet.

Frank spent his last few weeks of life in Freudenstadt. Peter was left with more responsibility than he wanted.

In the meantime another massive operation to reach the millions had been going on in South America, where a group of "changed" revolutionary Japanese Zengakuren students and their play "El Tigre" were attracting enormous crowds. They were led by a former Brazilian general through Brazil, up the Amazon, and were headed for Peru.

It was suggested that a Bingham would be helpful, since Father was so well-known there.

An evening in Rome, a glimpse of helmeted guards in Lisbon at midnight, and swarming attendants at Dakar found me the next day looking down on Rio's harbor, and on to Talara and Lima.

Without details of that campaign which enthralled me, I want to say I learned deeply to love the Latin Americans I met in Peru, Bolivia, Chile and then Brazil, each so different and each nation so different. Another friend who retains a special spot in my heart is Leonard Crane, a full-feathered Indian of the Canadian Northwest who always spoke his few words before mine—we stood together—at the end of each show.

Let us go on in our story, returning to Brickell warmed and enriched, to encounter an intensification of some of those elements which had surprised me at Caux.

Ray Purdy

You may recall the first man I encountered in MRA, whom I had met in my mother's home and followed around trying to show him how mistaken he was, was Ray Purdy, a dynamic, aggressive older man, who had spent most of his life since college working for the spread of Moral Re-Armament. I believe he had decided on a winning script from the positive material his parents had given him as a child. It was accepted, and he gave no contrary indication that he would have been a leading business executive or political figure if he had stuck to the "world" and its ways.

There had been persecution and bitter opposition from some quarters. This was regarded as the inevitable result of fighting for "change" and "remaking the world." The forces of evil were organized also. Ray was undaunted. His face shone. His smile was infectious. He dressed well and enjoyed the Cadillac a friend had given him, as he had no resources of his own.

Often in the development of the work he had been the American anchor man helping to find the financial or diplomatic support needed for extensive campaigns.

After Frank Buchman's death, he and his wife Elsa came to spend the winter in our home. I think he dreamed of reviving the airline sector which had languished, as I indicated earlier. Miami was also full of leading Cubans who had fled from the Castro regime. We made the acquaintance of many and tried to give them the ideology we felt they lacked.

It was a busy season of much work, much training. Like Buchman before him, Ray kept up an enormous correspondence. There were many film showings in our little gem of a theater. There were many dinners, many tea parties.

The ladies were not only expected to prepare the meals, but appear looking neat and well turned out with ideas as to what would be said, what stories told or films used. This was an obvious impossibility as I see it now with my Adult, but at the time, Ray was so sure, so radiant in his rightness that I always expected the miracle to happen the next time around.

Certain people yielded to change. Endless stories were told of these. Modesty was not permitted to hide these nuggets.

Bruce and I were uncomfortable hosts. We, too, yielded to the pace with the best grace we could muster. But too many of the strokes were conditional: You can be OK If . . . (you do as I say). Somehow Free Child was stirring; Vengeful Child was again raising his head!

Frank Buchman, though ill, had treated me with infallible courtesy when he was my guest. He battled for me to be *more* outgoing, to talk more.

By contrast, after the film showings in the evening, Ray would pull a chair out into the center aisle and talk for another half hour. It was too much. We felt it not to be right. Not all that many of the distinguished guests were accepting the offering.

My exchange of letters with Peter Howard proved to be a lifeline of hope. He said: "You have to be honest with what you feel. There is no other way."

It was not till spring and Ray was again going on his way that I gathered guts enough to express the negatives we had felt.

Ray's reaction to my letter wasn't clear. Obviously it hadn't made him happy. Looking back, I see that perhaps the most constant counterscript Driver for me is the Please Me one (Please the other person). I hate to challenge the other person face to face, and almost never do it. So I put my truth in a letter, justifying it by telling myself that he or she will have a chance to think it through calmly instead of reacting.

I satisfy myself that I've done something. But the spirit of the other must sense my lack of spunk and thus find an out in not taking what I say seriously. Certainly with all the thought-out letters I've written that way, the results over the years have been skimpy indeed.

On the other hand, the noncritical love I've managed to convey to people seems to have helped them in ways that words find difficult to define.

To convey something critical of the other person in order to set forth and defend my own position as I had had to do finally with Ray makes for a simple "crossed" transaction which cuts off exchange. Contrarily, to use and pin hopes on the issues between us being a lever to bring change to that other, which I have been attempting to do for years, turns out to be unrealistic and sentimental.

The results achieved by the fault-finding blasts of the Frank Buchmans and Ray Purdys of life may, as I've suggested, be the illusory fruits of the victim's Adaptive Child. They help to create organization, build up future opposition, and do not in the long run remake the world.

Poor indomitable Ray travelled triumphantly on for another year or so.

Though in the Transactional Analysis literature you will find the winners and losers sharply differentiated—it's obvious all of us want to be winners—I've come to feel the ironclad bind of a winning script is as difficult for the world to contend with as a losing script. There is something in the shock with which Ray met those last years that remind me of my own father's crushing final defeats.

Is it possible that with autonomy, I'm OK—You're OK, a winner can find it in his spirit gracefully to include and lead others into the positions he himself no longer seeks—*even if they're not doing things the way he or she would?* And he won't do it through Parent because he "should" or is told to. He'll do it because he loves the callow youth and others about him and *wants* them to take up their own reins.

Youth and Art Again

About this time Peter Howard was encouraging the emergence of new ways of reaching the world. I believe he was sensing the movement among youth that was to be known in the sixties as the "counter culture," well described in a humble book, Reich's *Greening of America*.

I went to Mackinac for the last time in the summer of 1964. Instead of the faithful adults that had borne the brunt of the effort of years there to reach minorities, industry, government, with a sprinkling of the young each year, this time Peter had insisted that the youth would carry the ball. A thousand of them transformed the atmosphere with a brash vigor that shocked our Parent ego states and tempted us to feel old-hat and unwanted. There were "hootenanies" of music so loud it shattered the eardrum. Vengeful Rebellious Child had full sway in the hallowed haunts where Absolute Purity had ruled for so long.

I made feeble attempts to fit in by shushing noisy onlookers standing outside the door to the main hall where youth delegations were taking turns in giving their convictions. But I was soon told my shushing was making more noise than those I had decided were interrupters. When a Miami delegation was called on to stand, I stood with the others and was laughed at by an old friend for a pretense at youth that my fifty-four years and white hair belied. The young people themselves were friendly.

This crowd was to flower by the next year after Peter's untimely death into what became known as Sing Out 1965 and the Sing Out movement.

However, I was glad to regain the family haven at Brickell Avenue.

Since responsibilities had become small and we were no

longer encouraged to take an active role in travel, I was delighted by the next year to take up painting again for the third time in life. My Little Professor welcomed as he had before the chance at my chosen creativeness, like a traveller in the desert revisiting a well-known oasis with its cool spring.

For almost the next five years I was free to pour energy through this channel. My art went to five continents and drawings shared in many a marriage festivity. Technically I had probably lost by the lack of attention to a craft, but spiritually I was freer to explore the ironic, the beauty in the midst of ugliness and commercialism, the universality of the divine in the ordinary that the intervening years had taught me to appreciate.

Blanton Belk and the Collapse of MRA in America

However, the weakening of the structure of MRA in America whose start Peter had somehow encouraged was proceeding apace. In the U.S., the older folk on whom the movement had depended for financial support and steady volunteer work, were in many cases discouraged, scattered and without links one with another.

The board of directors of the charitable corporation which gave a necessary legal skeleton on which to hang the muscles of all that went on were to follow the lead of an interesting high-powered individual named Blanton Belk.

While Peter in that last summer of Frank's life had been trying to give something new to the Americans, Blanton was co-leader of the mass moves in South America which I had joined. Occasionally Blanton would give me a positive stroke which thrilled me; at another time he blasted me publicly: "You're no revolutionary!" I was spending much money on advertising leaflets. I apologized without knowing much what I was apologizing for. Was I not Not-OK?

A handsome man with an extremely forthright manner and powerful voice, Blanton's ambition had led him to carve out a personal following among those whose basic life position, because of the MRA emphasis on sin, having necessarily been I'm Not OK—They (the leaders) are OK, were ready tools for such an endeavor.

In the years when Frank was alive, Blanton was one of the "bright young men" who, it was understood, were getting the training for the leadership of the future. He and his wife often publicly shared the blows to their pride that Frank's Critical Parent inflicted on them. We, the meek who listened, assumed this denoted acceptance and "change"!

We reckoned without the very thing that had been such a pattern in my own life, i.e., that while Adaptive Child openly conforms and obeys, Vengeful Child can collect abused feelings, bide its time and when the coast is clearer, cash in these trading stamps for a prize of revenge.

These changes were to be done in the name of "keeping up with the times." The "Spirit" could not remain bound by old patterns. However, much as I may agree today that the Spirit does constantly need new bottles, I believe Vengeful Child rationalizes the destruction it seeks rather than creating new forms which cherish the old even while outgrowing them as the Little Professor allied with Nurturing Parent may do.

Be that as it may, the structure split. The board authorized the creation of a new second corporation called Up With People, into which they funneled millions of the proceeds of the dismantling and disposal of the centers built with so much care over the years. This was to carry on the Sing Out movement with all the young.

A struggle ensued elsewhere. But the leaders in most of the rest of the world remained loyal to their existing concepts and each other. We shall see how I renewed my touch with them in further adventures.

Mother's Death, 1967

In writing about the life of one person, myself, I have necessarily neglected to give more than glimpses of the others in that life whenever they impinged upon me so forcefully as to create impact. These have been far from well-rounded portraits but more like news shots taken during stress.

During all the Moral Re-Armament years Mother had remained loyal, providing the quarters at Brickell Avenue. We, Brewster, Frances and I, saw her through the crises of old age, including the departure of Henry and her own declining health. Though she loved Connecticut and the beauties of her Salem "valley," during the cold months Miami and Coral Gables provided the amenities of better climate.

She had retained her fondness for music, playing with Henry into her nineties, and for discussion—with a slant favoring the incumbent president, whether Eisenhower, Truman or Lyndon Johnson. She had grieved over my divorce and favored my finding another person to comfort the latter years.

Eating like a bird, fastidious as ever, she slipped away in Salem, fully conscious almost to the last. This death had been so expected and thought about—she had often asked for it in her last months—that the memorial service was a joyful one of remembrance, uniting all the brothers as rarely during her life.

I didn't feel the need to grieve. The companionship that these years had brought seemed sustained. The old rebellions were long since gone as far as her person was concerned.

With Lucy to Spain

By now my children were well into their adult years and were to become close friends. I was beginning to reap the benefits of all the efforts at care that had brightened the last twenty years.

Though there had been times in Lucy's schooling when she had felt neglected and that I didn't visit her enough, she has let me know of my shortcomings so openly that our relationship has flowered. I may say she's become my sharpest and yet kindest critic.

How wonderful to feel I can learn from all my children instead of having them learn uniquely from me!

Norris had split from Wesley Fowler and was living in Spain. Lucy wanted to visit there, but anxious to see something of that country, would travel there with me first. It was one of the few great cultural reservoirs of Western Europe that I had never tapped, for which I'd often kicked myself. This was a glorious chance to go while on my way to Caux.

My curiosity, never sleeping much, had been working on the problem of what the rest of the Moral Re-Armament world was up to. We were told there was nothing going on and that Up With People were now the repositories of the spiritual energy with which the Almighty was bringing new ideas to the world.

We had been asked to put capital into a Life Income Fund, the proceeds to go to MRA after our death. Never before, though I had given hundreds of thousands to the work, had it been suggested that it was not needed right away for whatever buildings, campaigns or maintenance was the emphasis of the moment.

To the requests I had simply replied that I had no guidance to do it. No longer being included in activity had shaken my inclination to support in other ways. As you remember, it was the key words: "We need you" that had so captured me in the first place.

A middle-aged friend, himself torn, assured me that Caux was dead. But I would go see for myself.

We spent several weeks in Madrid visiting the Prado early each morning before the guided tours of tourists invaded those ineffable halls in their hordes.

Velasquez had always been a touchstone for me of grandeur mixed with the familiarity of paintings long known. However, in their huge size all together in considerable number, the effect was greater than I had expected. Confined as he had been to a restrictive royal court, his humanity and care for ordinary souls came through in power.

Nearby the less earthy El Grecos rose in spiritual ecstasy.

Then we hired a little Volkswagen and with my knees doubled under the dashboard, launched on a tour of road and countryside which would take us to such fabulous sights as Toledo and the Alhambra and through majestic barren hills before depositing Lucy with Norris in Malaga.

I went on to Caux by myself and sat through meetings absorbing the news that much was still happening in the old ways.

We had come through London on the way to Spain. It was obvious the team in Britain with their Westminster Theatre and busy houses in Berkeley Square and Charles Street were hives of activity.

While in Spain, careful to be in no designated MRA stronghold, I had written Blanton Belk a letter taking issue with him for the first time on domination as I had previously with Ray Purdy. No answer was to be expected, but these were the first stirrings towards climbing out of the position of I'm Not OK—You (the leaders) are OK. Where I would wind up was yet to be seen.

India

Lucy and I had enjoyed travelling together; we were ready to undertake a more substantial trip.

While at Caux I had renewed acquaintance with some of those from India, including Rajmohan Gandhi, grandson of the Mahatma, who invited me to come out to India to see what they were doing there. A center was being built at Panchgani outside of Bombay. A weekly news magazine, *Himmat*, was flourishing in Bombay itself. A travelling force, India Arise, with many dedicated young people, had not long before visited Europe. Asia where so many Third-World problems focussed, was the scene of fierce ideological struggles.

I had never visited the East, where so many of my brothers had been. It was time to do it. I went ahead to Bombay and Lucy followed as soon as vacation freed her. We were to have some months there with exceptional chances to meet Indians of all backgrounds and absorb as many impressions as possible of that rich, formidable, teeming universe.

For those who say and believe they want to "change the

world," to measure the extent of what that might mean it's important actually to see the lands where the millions are. We will never forget it.

India has often been described or written up. And truly that is one way in an effort to cope with the overwhelming sensations. I won't try to give more than a few snapshots. Everywhere we were met with the most gracious courtesy. And truly our hearts went out to all we saw, just as mine had in South America.

A harijan (formerly known as "untouchable") colony in New Delhi, where a man with a family and two little rooms had dedicated one of them as an MRA office. He had pictures around the walls; we sat on couches around the room and shared a Coke which represented close to a day's wages for him. Among those who spoke was an older man who staggered out in pain; he was just released from a hospital with cholera. Flies were everywhere.

Hundreds of children came to see us and sing. All the faces were loving and kind.

An upper-class cocktail party in Calcutta, scene of the unforgettable labors of "Mother" Theresa whose heart is big enough for even that dread-filled world. This party as far as the noise of chatter, the brassy self-assurance of the guests, and the tobacco smoke and alcohol might have been held in New York or L.A. Except that we were the only Westerners and a staple of the conversation was felicitating those who were managing to get their businesses out of the city and commiserating with those who couldn't. I had never experienced before such a doomed attitude.

Another scene in Calcutta was a tiny apartment on a side street. We visited a labor leader whose courage had been equal to facing an angry mob of fellow employees bent on violence. He, with his gracious grown daughters and wife, all squeezed into the little room, talked largely and cheerily of an answer for humanity.

Everywhere people, people, people! And though there were also surprising scenes of grandeur where nature was as wild as in one of our National Parks, the thing that lives in the memory is the kindness and breadth of the millions.

There was a whole bevy of young maidens who had dedicated themselves to MRA. Their simplicity of soul had attracted and charmed us.

Lucy, who is nothing if not sensitive and susceptible to atmosphere, had announced one day a decision more in accord with the same principles. They were thrilled and congratulated her so effusively that already she began to wonder whether she had meant as much as that.

By the time we returned to Caux, more doubts had come. Her grandmother, Norris's mother, was gravely ill in the U.S. She wanted to see her once again. Though she "didn't want to hurt" me, she was confident by that time that this had been a decision made to please, not from the heart's reality. She took off.

Fortunately what we had shared was important. I wasn't about to put pressure on conformities which had little to do with the person. My Nurturing Parent is not the tyrant that my Critical Parent has been.

Caux and the United States

I am sitting in the middle of a conference of extra importance. It seems we can no longer go along with the American leadership's claim that the Spirit had led them to break up the operation in the U.S. for the sake of a new approach.

A chosen hundred from all parts of the world, faithful over years, meet in a villa on the side by ourselves to decide what to do. How to reclaim lost ground? How to reestablish a moral position once abandoned?

Suddenly, secretly, two of the leaders, one Canadian, one British, take me aside. We will set forth for America as a nuclear force to do whatever is needed. I will be the American on the ground, as no move can be made there without at least one representative of the country most involved. The policy has been set; we will carry it out.

Without notifying others in Caux, we disappeared. A night or two in London to consult a legal friend. Then on to New York City and the entire U.S.A.

There was to ensue a fascinating few years of struggle and travel. I was to get to know many cities both in the United States and Canada, and make many more friends than I already had.

My Child was clearly pleased to be thus singled out and given such responsibility. True, Bruce, Frances and I had been among the few of the faithful who, living in the U.S. through the split, had yet maintained our links with London and Caux. I was freer to travel than they and had perhaps some organizational ability which would be helpful. The others of the handful of Americans there at that time had not been recently in the U.S., though soon they, too, were to assume obligation for the task of recovery.

Leadership and Organization

Though we were at first only three, we had many contacts throughout North America. Many of those we had known were, as I said, confused, loyal still in heart, and would rise to a renewed call for participation and action. The potential in terms of what had been may have been destroyed in buildings and equipment but was generous in terms of heart power.

Within a few years Canada was rewon and we were holding a continuing series of meetings in places like Trois Rivières, Montréal, Vancouver, as well as in the U.S. Delegations were coming to Washington, seat of power in this our troubled century. Some of the officials who had known MRA in its heyday, still spoke of it with respect. It was possible to hope that their longing for peaceful solutions would yet see that moral change was the only key thereto.

We formed our own lawful entity and were soon involved in heavy legal warfare, the American group having no intention of letting the territory go by default. This was to continue for some years till both sides were more or less exhausted and, without the victory or disappearance of either, accepted a certain status quo.

I had been elected by the board both executive director and treasurer of this new body, a concentration which I had sought to avoid but finally accepted as Child was gratified and Adult seemed to point out that that was a sensible if temporary solution.

After having been so involved in local organizations in Salem during my years on the farm, I had felt that organization was not a satisfactory way to carry on activity and make decisions. The people seemed always to get up against each other. MRA had showed another way through guidance and change, and this had seemed far better and more human. MRA. we were told, was not an organization but an organism, like a family, and this would obviate the frictions due to structure.

Our own split had shown this was not so true when character and basic They're-Not-OK positions collided. The fundamental problem, of course, remained—human nature and its proclivity for games.

However, I was not to hear of Eric Berne and the ego states for another year and it would be more than that before I could sort out the Not-OK elements in our own ranks; it was easy to see them in the ranks of the others.

So I had another chance at leadership—this time, though numbers were limited, on a continent-wide scale.

The script instruction: *You are shy—Children should be seen and not heard* was still operative. I had been around long enough to gain much personal freedom with others. But the minute a group was together, I backed off, collected feelings but came up with no worthwhile ideas. We in MRA often said: Any plan is stronger than no plan. I usually had no plan. *Living Statue* was still a reality. There was a curious blank.

Through the years with MRA I had developed letters as one wonderful way to get across life-changing ideas without having to use the tongue or voice box. These carried much of the fire that was denied me face to face in fact they generally were overcharged as vehicles for cashing in "brown" stamps. So I stuck to them.

Ideology

This is a difficult section for me to write, which I'd like to skip but can't without presenting an incomplete view of the movement to which I've given so many years.

I once went to see Frank Buchman in Mackinac in the years before he came to spend the winter in my home. I forget the occasion. It was considered proper to "check" with him before making any major move in one's life, like a trip or a marriage, to see what his guidance might be on the subject.

He was lying in bed. I repeated some words that were current then and which became the title of one of Peter Howard's books: "America needs an ideology." He sat up immediately, full of interest: "That's it! That's it!" If I were self-concerned about where I should go or what I should do, it didn't interest him. But when I echoed the theme of ideology, he came alive.

We had been given much instruction on the subject. Ideology was not just a philosophy explaining the world; it must be a consuming idea to which a person gave everything—time, money, life, which gripped every aspect of his thinking and doing. There were religions, there were faiths, but Moral Re-Armament was the only ideology the West had with which to counter Communism, the materialist one which had conquered half the world and was moving rapidly on every continent.

So far in this account I've steered away from the word "ideology" and only used it a few times, because I didn't want to get caught in the truth or falsehood of the foregoing. I'm writing up the adventures of my mind as it encountered subjective realities, not fixing once and for all the objective correctness of any theorem, least of all on such a slippery subject.

According to Peter Howard who had written "Ideas Have Legs" and for whom the World War years and the struggles between Naziism, Fascism and Communism had been full of lessons, the Communists were exercised over MRA and devoted time and effort to planning its destruction. According to that, the split that developed after his death and the breaking off of the American branch must have delighted them. It was perhaps fostered by them in ways which I couldn't fathom but some of my friends thought likely. Myself, I could explain the split more in terms of the characters of the protagonists.

Part of the Communist strategy would be to let MRA sink into obscurity after the weakening, so they wouldn't crow over the victory but simply ignore the whole subject.

We of the West and the Cold War years have had constantly to evaluate the reality of the Communist menace. We've been involved in some messy wars in consequence, and we've made mistakes. Hawks and doves both proclaim: We're OK—*They* are definitely Not OK, and feel hot about each other as well as about Communism.

Moral Re-Armament's claim to belonging in this league rested on the premise that the leaders of super powers could find change through moral standards, and with the Almighty's help this would enable them to establish new and friendly relationships with each other and thus avoid wars and their need. They could solve race and class differences and eventually all economic problems. I won't enumerate the impressive list of examples they have of this already coming to pass, except perhaps one: The outstanding rapprochement of France and Germany after the war through the efforts of Irene Laure, Robert Schuman and Conrad Adenauer.

Peter Howard's play, "Dictator's Slippers," visualizes this change happening in the upper rank of a revolutionary super power, thus putting the world on notice that in MRA's view such things were possible.

So theoretically they could be right. MRA could be a force to reckon with. Certainly God Himself if it is His chosen vehicle could use it for any purpose He wished. This belief has formed a mainspring of our activity. When my own direction began to diverge from it as we shall see, Bruce burst out in genuine desperation: "How could you desert us when the world is in such need?"

Paranoia

I know something of what paranoia is. I believe nations and movements can suffer from it as well as individuals. It's easy for my own mind to convert the negative forces my intuition senses on the outside into *all-powerful* magic ones.

For example, it's true Communism is potent and has made astounding gains in sixty years. The paranoid eye can easily project those gains into total takeover.

But like all human drives without much self-knowledge, it has borne within itself the same seeds of division which Frank Buchman sees so clearly in the materialistic West. China and Russia are far from united. Tito has maintained himself remarkably. New spinoffs exist and others seem imminent.

As a corollary to overemphasizing the negative, my paranoid mind can readily overemphasize my own importance in the eyes of those same negative powers. They may be ignoring me rather than moving to destroy me. In terms of strokes, those essential atoms of the human spirit, that is worse.

What I feel at this moment is that it's more important for me to see clearly what makes me tick and show it to others, than to diagnose the whole source and motivation of the destructive negative. There's obviously a lot of the bad in the world, a lot of violence, a lot of misery. However, when I am in the positive, the whole world is that much better off; it's a lever I have for changing it.

MRA says we need to do it together and I'm not effective if I do it alone. *I believe, however plausible that sounds, as it did for me for many years, that's the point at which the entity of organization gets back in!*

My Little Professor needs to take responsibility for the world. Okay! but creativeness, aliveness spring from within. "Checking" deadens and moves me from Spunky into Compliant

Child. I can lead by the attractiveness of my idea but not by the power of any office. The herd instinct and structure is out of date for rebuilding the world, at least as far as the craving for power goes, to be top dog or underdog.

Leadership—Bill Jaeger

Let's see how this worked out in practice when I was "on the road" once more—this time with a very few instead of hundreds, and this time close to the leaders if not, in truth, one of them.

The titles they had given me were nice, but in practice, as I've described, my "Be Silent" script meant that I was a figurehead, not an actual active leader. I did much of the solid work of keeping the accounts, arranging organizational details and paying for our travels. Beyond that others decided and others did the talking.

The American work had previously come to grief on the willfulness of those in the lead, who were most probably in the grip of Vengeful Child. What more natural than to encourage next a meek soul who couldn't speak up for his own ideas, who actually couldn't produce ideas of a strategic nature at all!

The two men I began to travel with have affected me deeply in these last years.

Bill Jaeger is a squat dynamo with an inordinate restless energy which helps to explain how he's gained top regard in the British team and worldwide. Of a working class background, he has a moving story to tell of early strife at home "which tore my guts," of a remarkable mother and how she began changing neighbors and hundreds of others after he met MRA at college in London and was honest with her.

He doesn't take kindly to any suggestion that there might be some unconscious scripting from this background. I believe his mother gave him some very positive feelings about himself which make any Not-OK aspects—or recognition of sins—fleeting and put in more for conformity's sake than strongly held.

He talks incessantly and well with an endless fund of stories both about our successes and the powerful threats on every side of the Communist conspiracy. He reads every newspaper he can get his hands on and many books and is always "in the know." This has baffled me for years and I've made ineffectual attempts to stem the flow and restore the balance.

With all this his personal care is magnetic; he is lavish with strokes, not all genuine but mostly so—so that I and others laughing tend to forgive the torrent: "That's just Bill."

I find it difficult to stay in Adult or perceive any objective truth when I'm with Bill. He plays: "My Information Is Better Than Yours" so vigorously that it hooks my Compliant Child nine times in ten. Thus his leadership asserts itself.

Claude Steiner, in writing about power plays, gives probably unwittingly the impression that they are evil, unusual, and to be contended with at all costs. I agree that I must be at all times alert to them and not yield when they appear.

However, being with Bill is like being subject to a continuous power play of his victorious nature. It will take the awareness that TA gives to keep me in Adult through that, otherwise I get resentful in Vengeful Child or go along submissively in Compliant Child. He is a lovable man, not a bad one—this makes it all the harder.

I have a document of statements made at Caux in 1952, a summer when change was really in the wind and all were touched by it. Bill Jaeger's analysis of what he does to others when he "knows best" was right on the mark as I've described it in my words. This shows that truth can come like a blinding light, we blink for a few months and then go on as before. TA has convinced me we must actually choose a new life position, I'm OK-You're OK before the Almighty can bring permanent change to use us as He wishes. Otherwise we play with change.

Leadership—Paul Campbell

The other friend will be even more difficult for me to characterize. Paul Campbell was for many years the closest person to

Frank Buchman as his personal physician, for Frank needed a lot of care in his last years. During the winter they spent in my home when Frank was so ill, Paul stayed on duty twenty-four hours a day for months.

He felt the most important thing he could do "ideologically" was to prolong Frank's working life, and this he certainly helped to do.

He has a sharp mind at the service of the twin constellation of Controlling Parent and Compliant Child. I believe his scripting was strict but positive and thus he tends to do well and take the lead in MRA.

Nurturing Parent doesn't come as natural to him as to Bill, and I believe somewhere his Critical Parent tends to criticize it as soft. He has a wife and two lovely daughters whom he loves, but when relaxing with them, some evidence would show he punishes himself for it.

A smoother, suaver man than Bill, he doesn't have the spontaneity. They work well together.

I cannot perceive any Free Child; it's rigidly restrained under the code.

The brilliance is turned towards the very strategic moves in which, as I say, I could come up with nothing. He was always three or four jumps ahead of us in terms of where we would go, whom we would see, where we would meet next, etc.

This I went along with for a while but finally found I could no longer, as we shall see. These moves always include guidance for others as well as himself.

He's genial and caring with me, but I think Critical Parent watches to see this doesn't go too far and give approval where it's not due. Thus he gives conditional strokes: You can be OK if . . . I'm uneasy as I used to be with my father.

Coauthor with Peter Howard of the life-changing textbook, *Remaking Men* (later issued under Paul's sole hand as *The Art of Remaking Men*), they postulate three main drives by which man's self will subverts the will of God. The three "Ss" are *sex, security and success.* Sex we would expect to see there as childhood scripts condemn it so strongly, as mine did. Success we have met under the heading "Mine Is Better Than Yours." Security, the materialist action of the Adaptive Child being concerned about money and survival, is characterized by fear—the very fear I knew so early.

According to the authors, the security-driven person shows a hardness and tightness of face which springs from fear, part of which is the fear of being found out, of being shown up not to be as capable as the person wants to be thought.

I've quoted the limerick about myself as a student: " . . . Your face is the face of a weasel . . . ", made during those years.

My stepfather, Henry, whom I learned to love, had such a tight face in his latter years. He often stifled a smile and found laughing an uneasy and rare happening.

Paul Campbell's look in repose can sometimes be called forbidding, though in command of himself in public, it shines with affability. My guess is that these shifts don't denote a fake but simply a shift of ego states. In his case the stoniness seems to reflect more Critical Parent than Spooky Child.

I submit that a scripted winner has just as hard a row to hoe as a loser. Since the types do not throng hospitals or therapy chambers, they may not be as well catalogued, but the world has occasion to know them well!

My friends gave me much food for thought. The back trap door, however, down which I often travelled after such meditations was: "I'm Not OK." It left me impotent to bring change.

PART III

TOWARDS AUTONOMY

CHAPTER NINE

I'm OK—You're OK

Explosion of Light

Just as one day on the farm, Norris had come along with an idea, "The trouble is we haven't loved him enough," which was to revolutionize my life, so almost casually was to appear in 1971 a fresh suggestion which was totally to shift what had seemed a fixed course.

Though I've given glimpses of the lives of my friends which perplexed me, I felt all that was needed was a further refinement of life-changing technique which would bring them to change, perhaps more honesty or more patience. Obviously those in leadership position couldn't be as quickly or easily shaken as those in some distress below.

But I had no inkling that a skylight would open in my own life and let in more illumination than it had yet known in all its sixty years.

I've always loved bookstores and no matter how "ideologically" dedicated I may be, I'll wander in and out to see what new thing may be presented. There one day the title, "I'm OK—You're OK," caught my eye. I was hooked as surely as any luckless salmon my son lures in the Pacific. I don't even remember what city it was in. By that time Miami was no longer much of a personal base; I was to spend more and more time in New York.

This book by Dr. Thomas Harris had already been out for some years and achieved a fantastic sale.

Like gulping fresh water in a thirsty land, amazedly I recognized the relevance of those TA conceptions I was meeting for the first time, to the issues with which I had struggled through a lifetime. In the introduction and, of course, throughout this book, you will recognize how much they've meant. The human soul is like an infinite well from which we can never tire of drawing more deeply.

I can only assume that my mind was hungry and prepared for new weapons with which to tackle the problems about which you've read. Moving closer to the inner circle in the world effort to recapture the U.S. for the "MRA" as traditionally practiced had fed my appetite for strokes but not satisfied me that I was being used as I should be. I had not yet learned to correlate fully what my eye saw with what my mouth said.

Perhaps my Little Professor was becoming wise enough to reach for his own nourishment.

Once again I became anxious to share a good thing I'd found with my friends and loved ones. It was fall—Christmas was not too far away. I went to the publisher and ordered three dozen copies so that I'd be prepared to spread them about as lavishly as wanted. Though I'd been disconcerted twenty years before by the less than enthusiastic response to MRA, this was different. Adult would be interested; there was no Parent: "You should," or "You must," which obviously had scared people before. Less than before would I be deterred by a turnoff. Many years had taught me: It's blessed to give and not to worry whether you're received.

Much Reading

This was not to be a one-shot deal nor the acceptance of a ready-made philosophy. The very fact that I was stirred by the intriguing new approach made me not only want to find out more but pursue what other comparable ideas were in the field. I had already been reading rather widely.

Lucy, in her own search, after India went to Esalen the next winter. She was full of encouragement, not so much for one system as for the new culture erupting in California, of which group therapy, Gestalt, the Carl Rogers School were all flourishing branches or aspects.

Reich's *Greening of America* had put into words what Nat and many friends had been preaching in action for decades, as he experimented in the Berkeley-Oakland areas with various life-styles before settling further north in Mendocino. I had followed his gyrations as well as I could with much tolerance and little information—often years would go by before I'd hear a word. I believe I recognized a Rebel Child at the core of his life, as there had been in mine, and it didn't particularly occur to me that this was the harbinger of a new way of life for all until Reich verbalized it.

This induced further exploration into such writings as those of Ken Kesey, Marcuse and Alan Watts.

Lucy gave me a copy of a Carl Rogers for Christmas as well as others. One of the most exciting of all these books was *Person to Person,* in which Barry Stevens, Carl Rogers and others had collaborated. Here more clearly than elsewhere could be sensed the split between a life of conformity through Adapted Child and the original autonomous life which Free Child—and Spunky—could give.

Simultaneously I began feasting on Eric Berne's own works and the related *Born to Win* by James and Jongeward. It seemed strange that Eric himself had passed on at the height of his powers. Claude Steiner has some moving thoughts on this in his own work.

You may wonder how I could do all this studying in the midst of incessant travel and seeing many friends. I was no longer an active householder. My colleagues had families—they had to be home at times. There were spaces between meetings. My work required many hours but not all. Correspondence was regular, not spasmodically demanding.

As I passed along the "Psychology" counters of the good bookstores I loved, twinges of guilt would say: this is not Absolute Purity, but the explorer already had the bit in his teeth.

Something hidden. Go and find it.
Go and look behind the Ranges—
Something lost behind the Ranges.
Lost and waiting for you. Go!

Whereas after reading Freud's collected works, it didn't take me long to find the way to a living disciple, A.A. Brill, and whereas Moral Re-Armament had presented its case with the smiles and song of active participants, I was in no hurry to contact TA people until I had picked the best of all these many "countercurrents." It's as though Adult already in reading about itself could say: take your time!

Eventually I got in touch with the Harrises and in October of 1973 without so much as a by your leave from my companions flew across the country to Sacramento to take part in a week's indoctrination workshop.

Sacramento

On a late hot afternoon with the sun beating down in a cloudless sky on what seemed a fertile plain at the edge of nowhere, I disembarked. My heart beat with the excitement of the unknown as I found my way to a motel on the banks of a muddy river across which loomed a few desultory skyscrapers. Instructions were waiting in an envelope with a questionnaire to fill out before we began in earnest the next morning.

I was happy to have a room alone, so I could rise early, have my quiet time, and have a quick swim in the pool as the same red sun quivered above the horizon. We were to eat all together and get to know each other at small tables as the days went by.

The mornings were for instruction. In rows as a classroom my classmates seemed exceptionally lively as ideas were bounced around. I was surprised how many games they seemed to know the names of. However, I didn't try too hard and trusted I would learn what I needed. Notes seemed too much, though I saw others busily taking them.

Afternoons were for group work where those things we were learning could be applied. We split into two groups of about fifteen each. There were no chairs but comfortable big cushions on the floor and we were encouraged not to make one nest but move around and relax with shoes off.

The leader of our group was a young staff member named Bob Miller, former engineer turned psychotherapist. He never particularly cottoned to me and an edge would appear in his voice as he twitted me about Moral Re-Armament about which he had soon learned. I may say this was good as he uncovered the role of my mother in my early script rather mercilessly and the Vengeful feelings which compassion might have encouraged me to hide. I enjoyed his freedom from Parent as he worked with the others.

As I've been to more workshops since then and studied the TA literature besides, I won't try to recall at what stage each element was learned or what seemed most important when.

It was fascinating getting close to such a varied group of young and old, men and women. Whereas the Harrises, Amy and Tom, only appeared occasionally and the two group leaders went home in the evening, we were together all day. In the evenings a few drinks mellowed friendships, though I didn't take one myself. I have never felt a personal need to lubricate warmth and haven't consumed one since 1951; I find it easy at bars to order ginger ales or "Virgin Marys"!

Each of the participants were searching, a few clergymen to freshen up their messages, most of us to freshen up our lives or marriages! One attractive dark-eyed girl, for example, sought strength with which to overcome the passive Child who found it too easy to let husband and others push her around. Another middle-aged divorcée, croupier in Reno, was competent and clever but needed strokes of love, not just sex. Young men, hostile or preoccupied, sought to find and build foundations for their lives.

I stayed on for a marathon (long-continued group session) at the weekend at which the other group leader, Craig Johnson, took equal part. More sympathetic to me than Bob, the two together with chair techniques and role playing penetrated further into my psyche and shed more light when it was my turn to "work" as they called it. Craig was an ardent, somewhat pop-eyed, young man pursuing a career and a doctorate through the new channels of studies of the mind, but he seemed to care.

Amy and Tom

When I went to Sacramento, Thomas Harris was just the name of a doctor and author. I had selected the Harris workshop out of the possible places to learn more because the book, *I'm OK—You're OK*, seemed to show a solid concern for the world, notably in Chapters 12 and 13, "P-A-C and Moral Values" and "Social Implications of P-A-C," that fitted in well with my own preoccupations.

The first surprise was to find not just one man but a husband-wife team. In his introduction and dedication Tom had given due credit to Amy for her collaboration, but I suppose like most readers I glance at introductory acknowledgements with no more than perfunctory interest as they seem always the same.

At some of our morning sessions Tom and Amy spoke together; at others Amy appeared with the younger men. I was impressed with the extremely lively humor that flew back and forth. Many points were acted out in living example.

On one of the evenings we were invited into the Harris home. On another Amy took us all on in a rap session at which any subject at all could be introduced. I soon gathered that she was a brilliant woman in her own right and that perhaps much of the orientation in the book towards religion and the world which had captured me was due to her inspiration and even writing. He struck me more as an amiable southern colonel (Texas, actually) who had strayed into psychiatry accidentally, thus surprising even himself.

The years with MRA and seeing people around the world had sharpened perceptions so that I would take no one on faith just because of the fascination of their doctrine, as I had so blindly twenty years before with the MRA groups. Somewhat disappointed with Tom, I yet said to myself: I don't need to go overboard in admiration; I'm here to learn and there is much to learn. The challenge is real.

Y

Each member of our group became fascinating as we got to know their lives intimately and not just from the outside. For years I had fantasized just such intimacy as giving the true strokes humans needed to give each other.

Y was a young woman clearly more disturbed than the rest. She had already been under treatment for some time at a well-known clinic—and was, I suppose, giving TA a whirl as one more approach. It seemed she had a close relationship to her father, severe parent, who had encouraged a Be Perfect attitude. The inability of life and what it gave her to measure up to perfection had evidently torn her apart.

Large of limb, the sight of her impacted me like a Greek goddess. For months I had been reading the psychic literature which assumed normal relations between women and men. It had undermined my dedication to the abstinence and chastity of the decades with MRA. What guidance I had encouraged me to move ahead without fear.

Here was an object worthy of compassion and love both. I rationalized an interest in one so much younger than I by thinking younger men would be scared by such unbalance, whereas with tolerance I felt I could easily deal with obvious Not-OKness. I had accepted the thesis that all could change life positions and no one was permanently "insane." Had I not been diagnosed as schizophrenic myself in the distant past?

I hadn't yet heard of the Karpman Triangle or the Rescue game!

At times, agitated, she would leave the sessions for minutes at a time. At others she would respond humanly to the dramas of the lives of others.

One day she threw a comment about "Mitch's beautiful

eyes." That clinched it! On the last day as we stepped along the walkway outside the rooms, I said something about marriage. She said quickly: "We'll have to write each other."

I wasn't surprised to find that I had said what I did. Though it was in total contrast to all the behavior and attitude of the MRA years and as well to the shyness and restraint of the pre-MRA years, Free Child was out and though not thought out in Adult or restrained by Spooky, it felt good.

To explain further, I must add that part of what we had been learning was a freedom to give physical strokes—in this case limited to decorous hugs. We had recessed at times for other bodily exercises involving trust in each other. Some of the individual "work" was also done in corporeal terms like battling with bataca gloves, or etc.

But my action went beyond those things and affirmed a new OKness and willingness to risk.

Euphoria

I left Sacramento in an exalted state. I'd been shown the possibility of living up in the I'm OK—You're OK quadrant where lots of strokes are available and the feelings can be expressed by: "Wow!"

Rather than rush back to the East coast, I needed time to absorb the radiance. A workshop can be physically exhausting. There was Nat to see nearby in California, and my granddaughter Jalena. I wanted to hug my whole family now that I knew the value and necessity of physical strokes beyond the verbal ones I had usually been giving.

Even on the short plane ride to San Francisco I was "high"—each person I caught sight of seemed incredibly important and I fantasized pleasant encounters and did get a smile or two.

The big moment came in the dome house Nat had built himself up in the "pigmy" forest of Mendocino. I embraced him so warmly that years of difficulty dropped away. Jalena wasn't having any—"Don't do that," as she gave me a signal that all was nevertheless well. (A child can transmit in a second an indication of whether she's OK or not.)

Kathy, the warm person who was Nat's "old lady" at that time, greeted my clasps with pleased giggles.

After a time it remained clear they all approved highly of the change. Nat himself had just been going to some local group sessions, so it was easy to exchange good impressions.

Through long mornings at the motel I stayed in and watched the tops of the heavy waves curling beyond the shore meadows. Though it was cool outside as I walked around, the contrast was strong between the euphoria of those days and the puzzlement I had felt alone on Key Biscayne twenty-two years before as I thought out an adjustment to the preferred MRA position of I am Not OK—You (the leaders) are OK.

In many years of Bible reading I'd often come across the phrase: "Love thy neighbor as thyself." Only now was I beginning to learn what "as thyself" might imply.

By the time I was back in New York, I was writing the "Aphrodite" Y some ardent letters. It was a joy to express warmth as I hadn't done for many years.

Her reply was curt and to the point. There was to be nothing between us.

However disturbed she might have appeared when observed at the workshop, she showed a shrewd, compassionate intelligence in thus warning me not to get hooked onto a hopeless cause.

Though I wrestled with it in my mind and wondered why, there seemed little use spending energy on it.

Q

Continuing travel took me home to Miami. One evening, visiting with the caretakers, Mr. and Mrs. Lawrence, with whom I'd become firm friends, I found a casual lady visitor, Q.

Somehow the tempo picked up. Some electricity got into the

air as actual banter came into the conversation. The Lawrences were surprised that my usual fairly serious talk had given way to Free Child excitement and laughter.

Q had been married, had a good job in Texas, was not as young as Y.

Child had found another person with whom fun was to be had. However, by the next evening, though I had a suspicion she would be waiting for me to make a move, the old blocks returned. Some story went through my mind that I mustn't give way too easily to an attraction. In TA terms that didn't make sense as I was looking for fun and not risking anything. But Parent doesn't give up its Not OK control all at once without a struggle, without ups and downs!

By the third day she had gone. However, I initiated correspondence and was delighted to get a positive letter back.

Before too many months I was touring Texas, and though I made some good calls on the way, the real objective was El Paso, where Q lived.

The new freedom I'd found at the Harris workshop had obviously uncovered a long-buried desire for feminine companionship and closeness. Though I was to seek fervently for the right person, inexperience couldn't prevent several tries which didn't work out before the final success.

Looking back now I'm grateful that God has given me several friends, each of whom has enriched my life. Q would no longer say she was a friend, but at the time she responded.

My life, especially under the MRA aegis, had been ruled, as you've seen, by the injunction: You will *Never* attain. Love is OK but sex is a No-No! That was beginning to break down as my search began. However, the script of the other person must always be considered as to what kind of transactions there will be.

Though at first our connections had been such good Child-Child ones, and letters had been encouraging, I found a person with an injunction the reverse of mine, i.e.: Sex is OK; Love is a No-No! Love is too threatening and closeness—which means intimacy, not just physical contact, is to be avoided.

Surprise! I soon left under a barrage of criticism. And though I was to try again and even met Q in another city, the pattern wouldn't break. The closer I got the more I got bombarded.

Blessed Q. I cannot get vengeful over your hangups! Crossed transactions were bound to come. I want intimacy and not games!

Development

In order to continue and widen my reading of TA material, I subscribed to the TA professional magazine, the *ITAA Journal.* There I found an article on the "Miniscript" by Taibi Kahler and Hedges Capers which included the postulates about the "Drivers" and the "Allowers" (described in the introduction).

This excited me as giving more insight into the day-to-day workings of the human spirit. I felt I wanted to meet and learn from these men who formed a common "institute" at that time in La Jolla, near San Diego. I drove down there, met and responded to Betty, Hedges' wife, and arranged to attend a three-week "summer" workshop in June.

Again I was reaching into the unknown led on by the passion for light.

When I first caught sight of Hedges Capers, grinning with a lei around his neck and surrounded by admirers, I thought I was seeing a Roman emperor come to life. He turned out to be a nurturing, warm-hearted man around whom seemed to spring miracles of change and new life as he lived in I'm OK—You're OK. No wonder he was loved and sought after.

Beyond the more usual group sessions in the mornings, we were encouraged to work closely in a small group of three in identifying the specific elements of our scripts, working with comprehensive questionnaires which we took turns in asking each other. I was fortunate to find myself with a couple of lively young people who welcomed my participation.

However, my attendance for the three weeks was interrupted in a surprising way. A free crowd, some of us had paid a visit one afternoon to Black's Beach below the cliffs of La Jolla, which is one of the few permitting nude bathing. This, which only months before I would have found disturbing, I was now pleased to join without strain.

I was determined to go again and did so, but the second time the consequences were not so pleasant. For many years I had suffered from hemorrhoids but managed to control them myself without needing medical care. It had been an embarrassment though I had known a good many friends go through operations for the same thing.

That second swim in the rough cold water was too much for the condition. By the next morning I was in a hospital preparing for surgery.

As I thought about it in bed and went through the before-and-after rituals, I realized that Be Strong had been one of my drivers, though unadmitted, which had kept me from recognizing or yielding to pain—"Don't Feel." Here in this vivacious company, with each of us clarifying our own scripts, I had gotten so free that I no longer had to "Be Strong" about the piles. I could have them dealt with and really overcome, not just covered up in pretense.

Lucy was kind enough to receive me in her home in L.A. for the convalescence. Although my formal training had been interrupted, I was gaining more OKness all the time!

Naomi

One of the best things to come out of this workshop for me was a friendship with Naomi S. I had been attracted by her liveliness and enthusiasm during those days; I wrote from Lucy's to see if she could meet me for an hour at the airport on her way home to Florida.

She had had a remarkable struggle to achieve OKness. Deserted in childhood, her mother institutionalized, she had had to contend with strong feelings that somehow it was all her fault. She had decided to nurture the other children when confined with many parentless waifs. Thus a natural bubbling spirit which yet overlaid dark shadows that TA was helping her to uncover and deal with.

I made several trips to Florida to see her and meet her two

delightful children. There I heard more about her childhood and the pitfalls of her marriage and divorce.

She was grappling with her destiny courageously in spite of drawbacks that might have embittered another person. This led to social work, counseling in schools, and eventually therapy clients of her own. The decision to be in Nurturing Parent was still a guiding one through life.

Intellectually we got on well and became fast friends. In other ways—Child-Child, for example, the relationship didn't get off the ground. Though we gave ourselves *permission* in Adult, there wasn't the deep underlying hook which seems to be necessary as a base for a closer woman-man tie.

I didn't find this hard or painful as, for example, my battles with Norris had been where I was hooked into the Rescue Triangle. Wonderful nourishing strokes of OKness can yet come from such a friendship where sexual intimacy is not a factor.

One thing Naomi was to say in prognosis of any closer bond: "We're two leader types. I don't think either of us could play second fiddle to the other."

I was happy to concede that that was true for her, and that she couldn't be content to follow me around when she had a career and a vocation to pursue. But it hadn't struck me that I was much of a leader. Adult accepted it as a word in connection with my work responsibilities, but the Little Professor in Child insisted: you never have been able to lead others—you're lucky enough if they catch some ideas you've spread before them. You don't want to push ideas onto others now, even if you could.

Naomi was to do me the honor of visiting me in New York also. We had a fun time, but the mysterious hooks didn't appear there either. I'm grateful that this kind of friendship can exist in this age which would have been more difficult in another.

Aloneness

I was happy to have had these various contacts with women—all exciting and different after so many years of propriety.

Now that I had broken the ice, the floodgates were opened and I was determined to find the right person with whom I could really experience intimacy and garner all kinds of good strokes.

New York City with its millions seemed a good place to do it. Miami hadn't fostered many new friendships through the years when I was painting there again.

I had a tiny room high aloft looking up Lexington Avenue to the spires of the Chrysler and Empire State Buildings. I loved the streets with their multitudes and the subway filled with personalities most of whom seemed to live under dark shadows but with its own quota of youth and charm.

Humanity, ground down by a monstrous city, yet survived in its dramatic splendor.

The numerous friendships formed under the aegis of MRA which formed the staple of my day-to-day life, were oriented in one direction only and couldn't be used for a different purpose.

I was at a loss and again after many years felt sharp pangs of aloneness. It was bearable—I knew what I was after—but once Tantalus has tasted the grape and cooled his tongue in the water, to have them again withdrawn, even if temporarily, has its own special ache.

Lucy advised me that I was inexperienced in meeting the ordinary person and going about it wrong. People are afraid to be approached cold in a civilization where violence captures the news and the imagination of men.

I forced an exchange or two but was too tense to have them flower. Shyness is not just an attitude but circumstances I limit myself with.

Thus, though TA was bringing a new life, it couldn't all be champagne. Temptations were strong at times to feel Not OK.

Reaching Others—Al

However, one of the greatest joys through those days was being able to reach a few of the young with honesty about what I was learning and a sympathetic ear for their ups and downs.

I had known Al since his early teens in Miami. He had been in the army in Germany and married there. Now they had two lively kids. Without a heavy education, yet Al liked to talk and think out what was going on in the world.

We had a common background of Moral Re-Armament chatter and friends. He, too, was dissatisfied and not ready to line up with an authoritarian group or preestablished ways.

When we went to a small conference of many of our old friends, we were startled to hear a speaker say: "There's too much reading going on of psychological books." This with its echoes of all the Parent prejudices of the past, of the Inquisition or the MGB, only confirmed what we were beginning to see, that a Parent-dominated organization is not enough to cure the ills of the world, no matter how virtuous.

In specific TA terms, if all or most of the followers of an organization are encouraged to be in Adaptive Child—I'm Not OK; You're OK, I'll follow you—there cannot be the creative thought necessary to deal with the real world. Only souls who can roam the realms of thought freely can come up with light and fire enough to tame the destructive demon in man.

I think of all the friendly folk whom I have visited over the years, with whom I've talked and to whom I've wanted to give something. Endless opportunities, thousands of meals with the fascination of all that's said. Life-changing has always been in mind, but nothing pushed, nothing overemphasized. In these more recent encounters, especially with these youths, a more relaxed attitude may have allowed the Almighty to go further than ever before.

Reaching Others—X and Z

One day Russell told me of his distress after seeing one of his young cousins. Although married with babies and a good career opening up, X was deeply depressed and had been for some time. Here was an obvious need which maybe I could help meet.

I took a train to the city where he lived and worked and

spent the evening talking with him and his wife. From a relationship which before that had been only casual grew a closeness which has been marvelously rewarding.

He told me much of his life. Grown up on "easy street" with provident parents and a loving, nurturing grandfather, he yet hadn't found enough strokes with which to build confidence and a faith.

I can't violate confidences to relate some of the high points, but here was a clear case where some wrong script decisions had been made. The incidents were subjectively painful; viewed objectively, they didn't seem all that serious. However, the resultant life decision was devastatingly somber: I'm Not OK—You're Not OK.

Although he had been treated in psychoanalysis for some years, he grew excited as I outlined the TA approach. A new hope had appeared on the horizon.

He was to devour the books I gave him and decided almost immediately to use his two-week vacation to attend a workshop in La Jolla with Hedges Capers.

The results, I may say, have been transforming. Not all the events have been harmonious or wish-fulfilling. It may never be that we find a new dynamic in our own lives without disturbances in the lives around us. But he is taking charge in a new way and *feels* different, as well as looking and acting different.

His gratitude to me for helping find this is one of the precious things in my life.

These touches made me feel good. Not all were so satisfying.

I went down to a southern city for a week, where my colleagues were making the biggest effort to restore the traditional MRA team, to see a young woman, Z, who had shown serious signs of derangement and seemed headed for hospitalization.

Here, in spite of the courtesy and graciousness of my welcome, there was no sign on the part of her parents that what I had to say or give would be of value or worth serious consideration. The poor girl, a lovely person, was polite and perhaps amazed that anyone would make such an effort for her. She didn't seem to take in much of what I said. I felt pain and that that endeavor had been a waste and a failure.

But some months later I received from her a chatty letter full of news which began as follows: "When anybody tries to help somebody as uncooperative as I was and then cares enough to write them almost twelve months later, I can assure you it is no difficulty to reply . . . "

It's evident that for the moment she has found a situation in which life is not too bad after all.

The Almighty weaves the fabric of events around each life. I would never be able to prove that anything I did had a part in this stabilization. But proof or no, I'm convinced that an act of compassion is never wholly lost. It seems to touch events in ways that defy control or scientific evaluation.

Power Struggle

I was to attend another couple of TA workshops, a big ITAA conference. My search for a companion and wife was to continue till I began to woo Hilda.

Gradually a sense took hold of me that I must sever the active connection with the friends with whom I'd been working for over twenty years. Though I hadn't approved of the spin-off of the US group, I couldn't in conscience continue to hold a post of leadership in reconstruction when I no longer approved of our own methods or actions.

You will have gathered from page to page how my conviction gradually formed that any organization along traditional lines is not the way. Somehow inherent in Parent, inherent in the pursuit of power which every individual in that ego state seeks to impose wherever he or she can, is a disregard of the unique in the other person in spite of all the disclaimers which our modern age has taught us. I believe power was imposed with a better conscience in past times where Parent held more obvious sway.

I began to put these new views into action and take the necessary steps of resignation.

Much was focussed in a weekend spent in New Jersey in the spring of 1975. Here was gathered a group of old and good friends. Plans were to be made for the future. Though unsaid, I'm sure the thrust of effort was to lead me back into the fold along the well-known paths.

I cannot pretend all the issues were stated as I have in these pages. I was able to expose the feelings of unease which had so often remained hidden.

As one example, I sought a strategy for the winning of the Communist leaders whose destructiveness we so often decried. If our ideology was for everybody, as we maintained, was there no plan to meet and change these men who so often seemed in our eyes the epitome of evil? They had been changed in the Ruhr in the fifties, and elsewhere. What about now?

At mealtime almost everyone gave me strokes on how refreshing and challenging the ideas I expressed were!

However, I had the desperate feeling that no matter what I said, they couldn't agree.

Only now can I sense that I was seeking my own power in a group where lines of power were long since established.

Weeks afterwards I learned one or two of my ideas had made some headway. The substance was never the real issue. The issue was not only who was in control, but that lines of control do exist.

What about God, nominal chief of all our endeavors, to whose voice we listen every morning and whenever we need to together? Each one went away from that weekend convinced that he or she had God on their side. I suspect that He smiled at us in His Mercy.

He had created us—or we had evolved—with the capacity for different ego states and life positions. We could be in: I'm OK—You're Not OK and play War!

Or we could be in: "We're OK—You're OK *if* you're fully with us.

Or finally we could be so free as to believe and say: We're OK—You're OK anyway. God has left *us* free to choose; you can be, too!